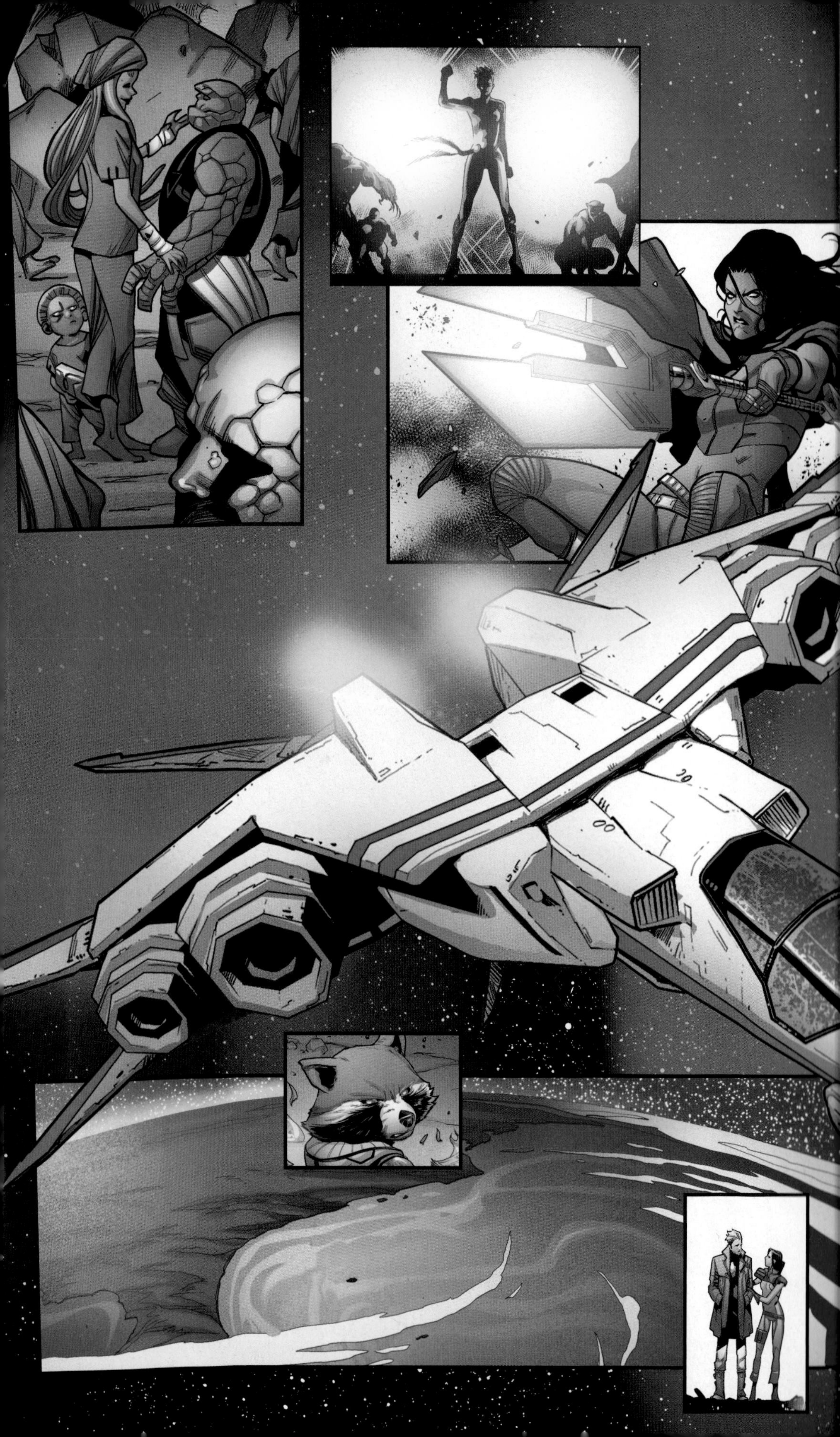

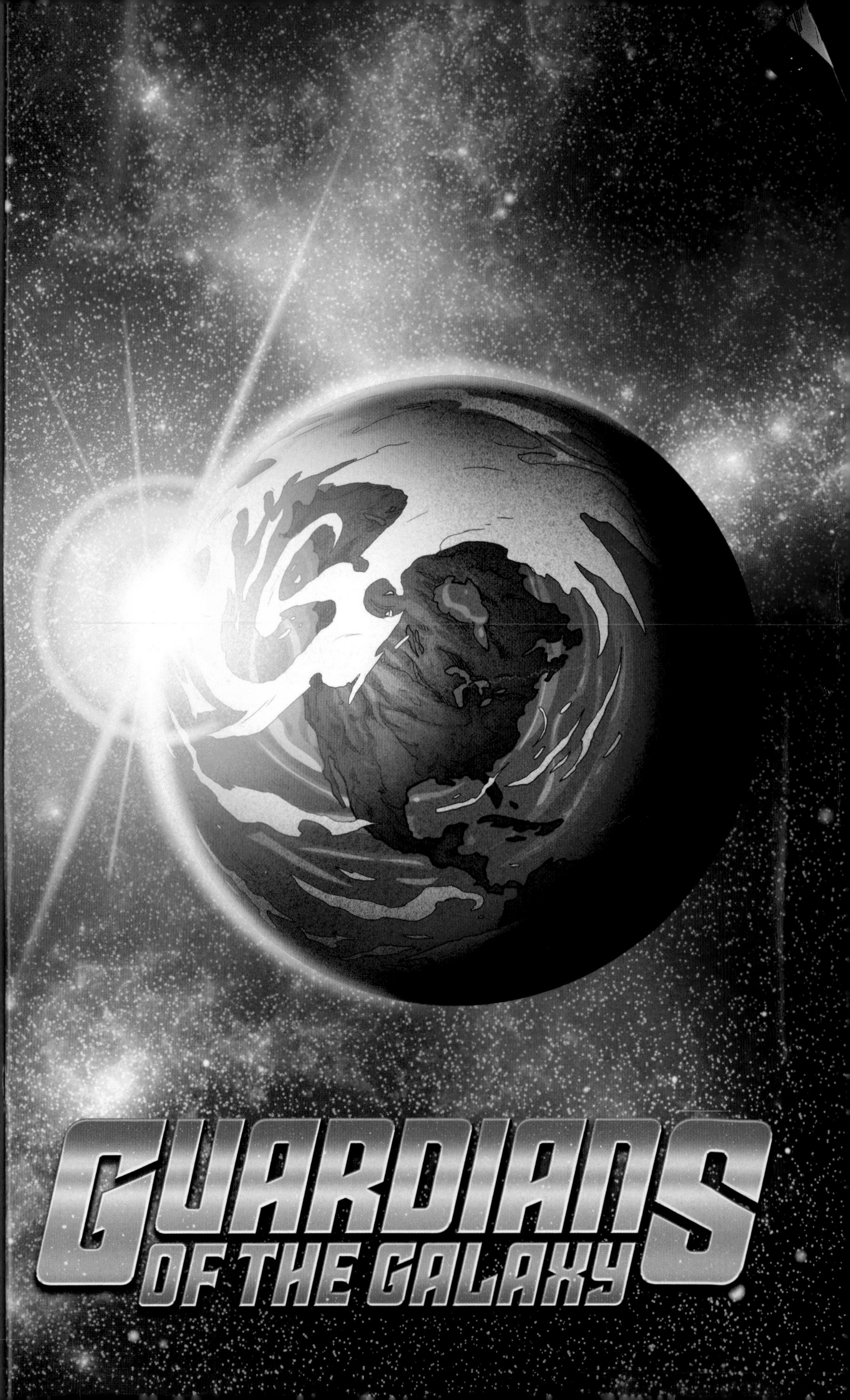
GUARDIANS
OF THE GALAXY

GUARDIANS OF THE GALAXY

OF THE GALAXY

CIVIL WAR II

BRIAN MICHAEL BENDIS
WRITER

VALERIO SCHITI [#11-13]
& KEVIN MAGUIRE [#14]
ARTISTS

RICHARD ISANOVE
COLOR ARTIST

VC's CORY PETIT
LETTERER

ARTHUR ADAMS & JASON KEITH [#11-13] **& KEVIN MAGUIRE** [#14] COVER ART

KATHLEEN WISNESKI
ASSISTANT EDITOR

DARREN SHAN
ASSOCIATE EDITOR

JORDAN D. WHITE
EDITOR

FREE COMIC BOOK DAY 2016

JIM CHEUNG
PENCILER

JOHN DELL
INKER

JUSTIN PONSOR
COLORIST

VC's CLAYTON COWLES
LETTERER

JIM CHEUNG &
JUSTIN PONSOR
COVER ART

ALANNA SMITH
ASSISTANT EDITOR

TOM BREVOORT
WITH **WIL MOSS**
EDITORS

COLLECTION EDITOR: *JENNIFER GRÜNWALD*
ASSISTANT EDITOR: *CAITLIN O'CONNELL*
ASSOCIATE MANAGING EDITOR: *KATERI WOODY*
EDITOR, SPECIAL PROJECTS: *MARK D. BEAZLEY*
VP PRODUCTION & SPECIAL PROJECTS: *JEFF YOUNGQUIST*
SVP PRINT, SALES & MARKETING: *DAVID GABRIEL*
BOOK DESIGNER: *JAY BOWEN*

EDITOR IN CHIEF: *AXEL ALONSO*
CHIEF CREATIVE OFFICER: *JOE QUESADA*
PUBLISHER: *DAN BUCKLEY*
EXECUTIVE PRODUCER: *ALAN FINE*

GUARDIANS OF THE GALAXY: NEW GUARD VOL. 3 — CIVIL WAR II. Contains material originally published in magazine form as GUARDIANS OF THE GALAXY #11-14 and FREE COMIC BOOK DAY 2016 (CIVIL WAR II) #1. First printing 2017. ISBN# 978-1-302-90301-5. Published by MARVEL WORLDWIDE, INC., a subsidiary of MARVEL ENTERTAINMENT, LLC. OFFICE OF PUBLICATION: 135 West 50th Street, New York, NY 10020. Copyright © 2017 MARVEL No similarity between any of the names, characters, persons, and/or institutions in this magazine with those of any living or dead person or institution is intended, and any such similarity which may exist is purely coincidental. **Printed in the U.S.A.** ALAN FINE, President, Marvel Entertainment; DAN BUCKLEY, President, TV, Publishing & Brand Management; JOE QUESADA, Chief Creative Officer; TOM BREVOORT, SVP of Publishing; DAVID BOGART, SVP of Business Affairs & Operations, Publishing & Partnership; C.B. CEBULSKI, VP of Brand Management & Development, Asia; DAVID GABRIEL, SVP of Sales & Marketing, Publishing; JEFF YOUNGQUIST, VP of Production & Special Projects; DAN CARR, Executive Director of Publishing Technology; ALEX MORALES, Director of Publishing Operations; SUSAN CRESPI, Production Manager; STAN LEE, Chairman Emeritus. For information regarding advertising in Marvel Comics or on Marvel.com, please contact Vit DeBellis, Integrated Sales Manager, at vdebellis@marvel.com. For Marvel subscription inquiries, please call 888-511-5480. **Manufactured between 12/16/2016 and 1/30/2017 by LSC COMMUNICATIONS INC., SALEM, VA, USA.**

10 9 8 7 6 5 4 3 2 1

FREE COMIC BOOK DAY

CIVIL WAR II

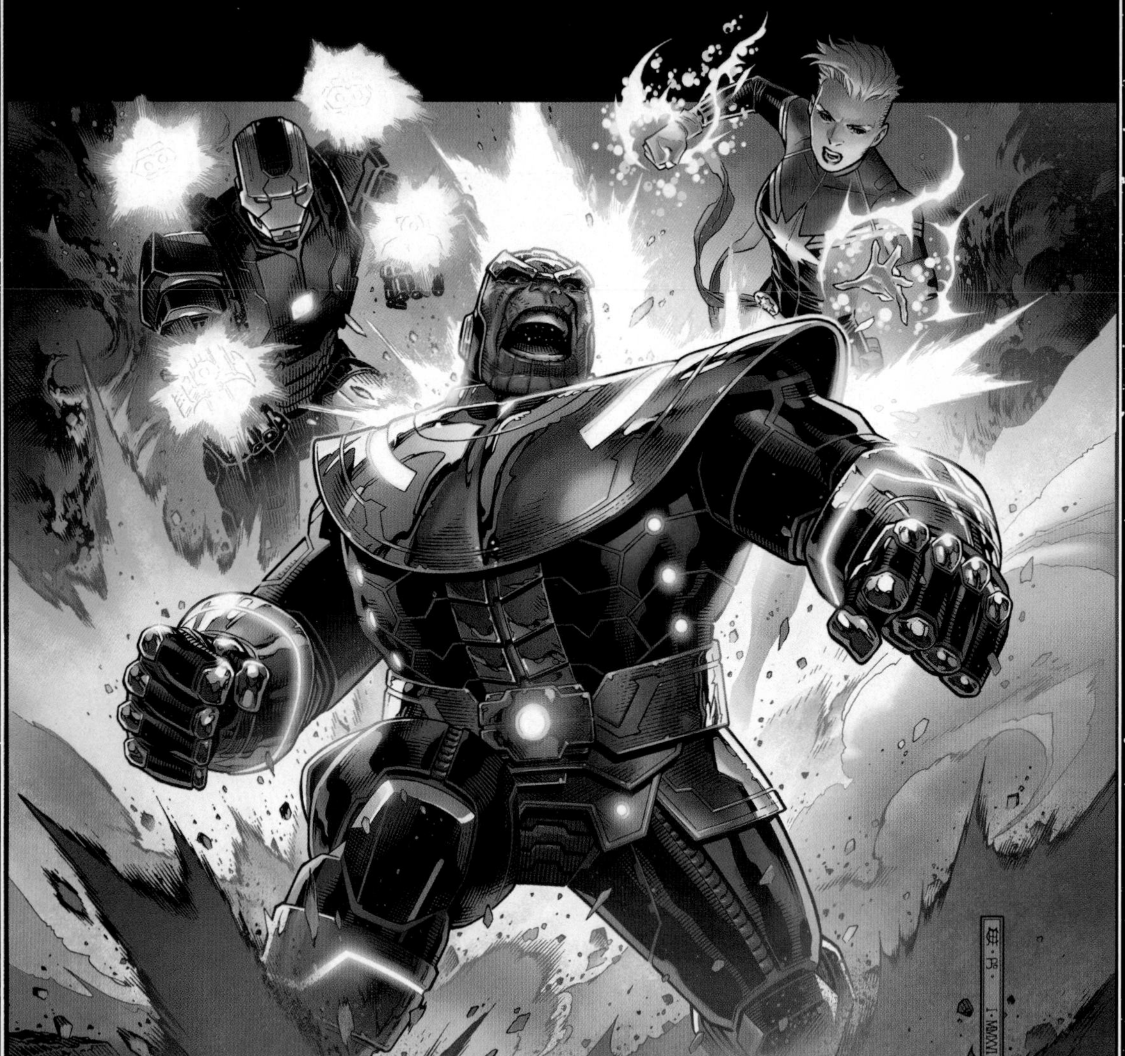

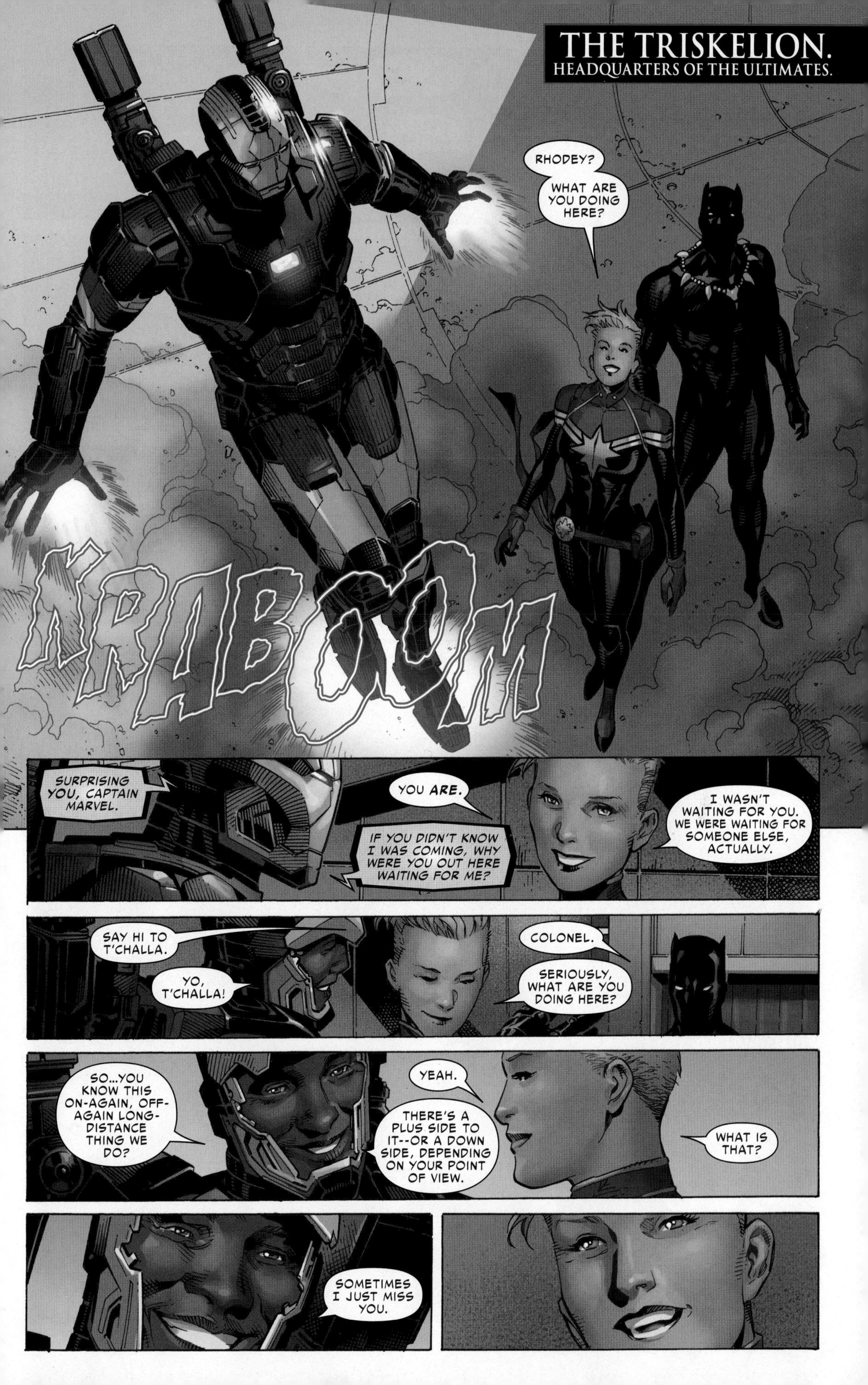
THE TRISKELION.
HEADQUARTERS OF THE ULTIMATES.
RHODEY?
WHAT ARE YOU DOING HERE?
KRABOOM
SURPRISING YOU, CAPTAIN MARVEL.
YOU ARE.
IF YOU DIDN'T KNOW I WAS COMING, WHY WERE YOU OUT HERE WAITING FOR ME?
I WASN'T WAITING FOR YOU. WE WERE WAITING FOR SOMEONE ELSE, ACTUALLY.
SAY HI TO T'CHALLA.
YO, T'CHALLA!
COLONEL.
SERIOUSLY, WHAT ARE YOU DOING HERE?
SO...YOU KNOW THIS ON-AGAIN, OFF-AGAIN LONG-DISTANCE THING WE DO?
YEAH.
THERE'S A PLUS SIDE TO IT--OR A DOWN SIDE, DEPENDING ON YOUR POINT OF VIEW.
WHAT IS THAT?
SOMETIMES I JUST MISS YOU.

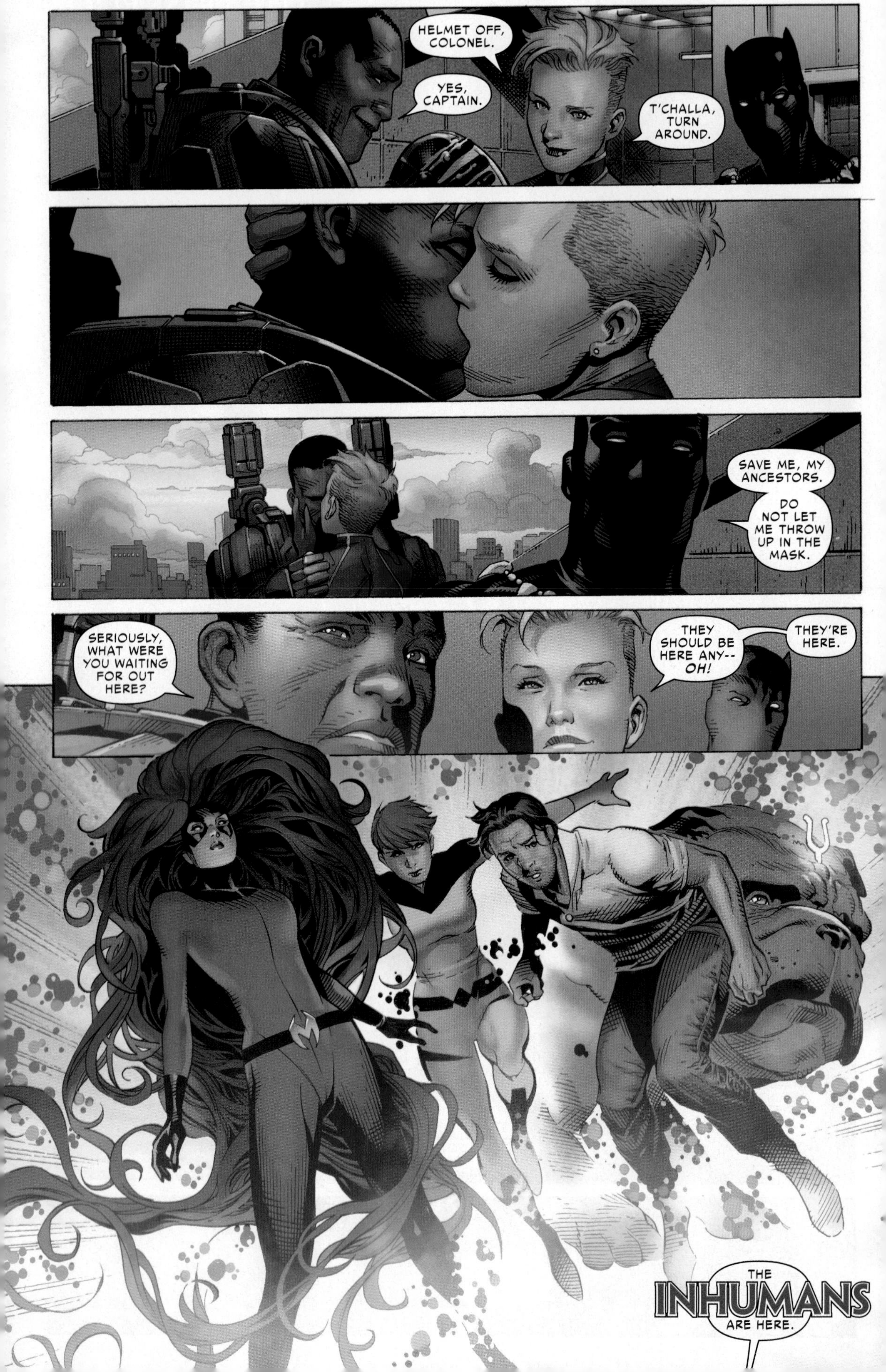
HELMET OFF, COLONEL.
YES, CAPTAIN.
T'CHALLA, TURN AROUND.
SAVE ME, MY ANCESTORS.
DO NOT LET ME THROW UP IN THE MASK.
SERIOUSLY, WHAT WERE YOU WAITING FOR OUT HERE?
THEY SHOULD BE HERE ANY-- OH!
THEY'RE HERE.
THE INHUMANS ARE HERE.

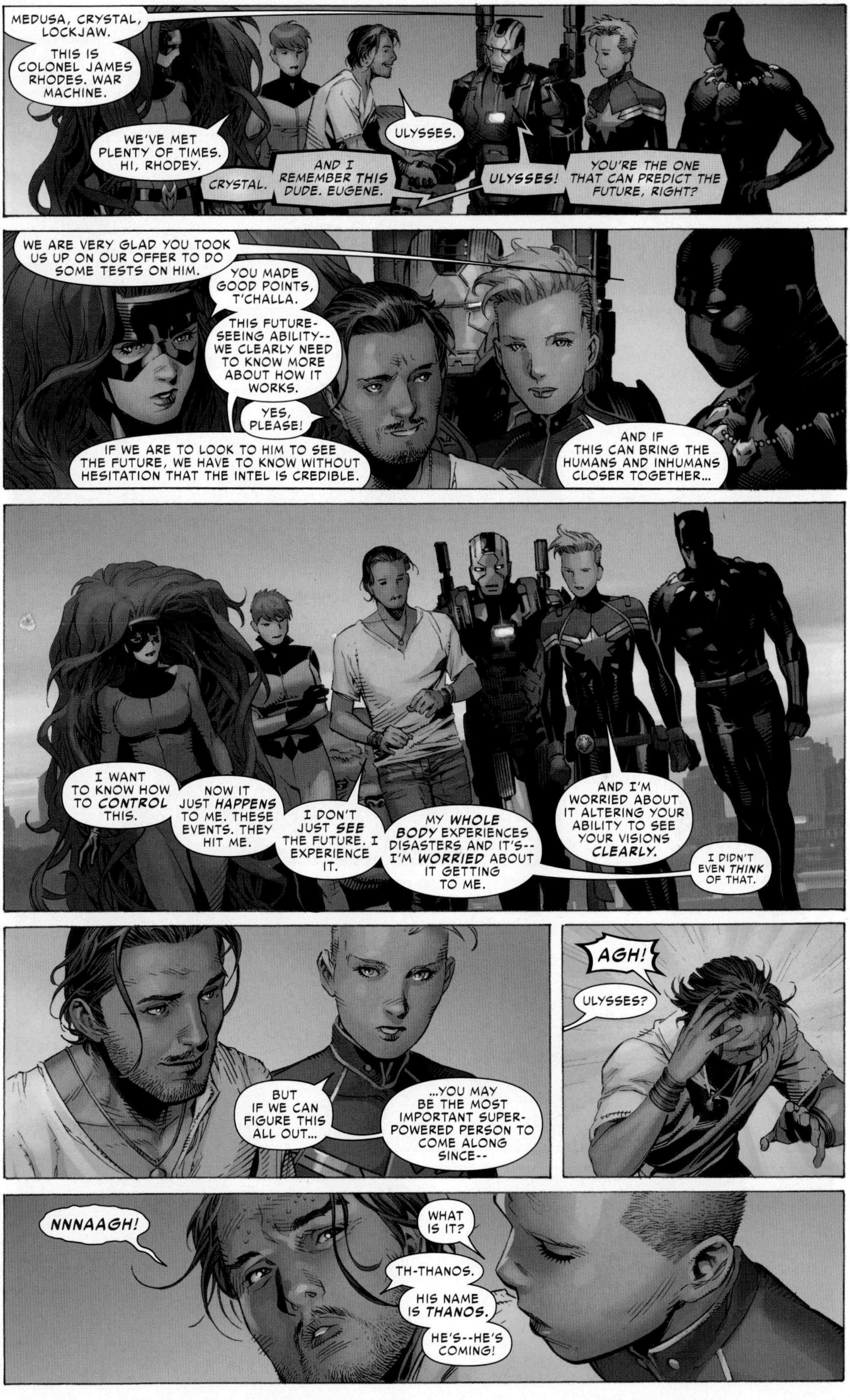
MEDUSA, CRYSTAL, LOCKJAW.
THIS IS COLONEL JAMES RHODES. WAR MACHINE.
WE'VE MET PLENTY OF TIMES. HI, RHODEY.
ULYSSES.
CRYSTAL.
AND I REMEMBER THIS DUDE. EUGENE.
ULYSSES!
YOU'RE THE ONE THAT CAN PREDICT THE FUTURE, RIGHT?
WE ARE VERY GLAD YOU TOOK US UP ON OUR OFFER TO DO SOME TESTS ON HIM.
YOU MADE GOOD POINTS, T'CHALLA.
THIS FUTURE-SEEING ABILITY--WE CLEARLY NEED TO KNOW MORE ABOUT HOW IT WORKS.
YES, PLEASE!
IF WE ARE TO LOOK TO HIM TO SEE THE FUTURE, WE HAVE TO KNOW WITHOUT HESITATION THAT THE INTEL IS CREDIBLE.
AND IF THIS CAN BRING THE HUMANS AND INHUMANS CLOSER TOGETHER...
I WANT TO KNOW HOW TO CONTROL THIS.
NOW IT JUST HAPPENS TO ME. THESE EVENTS. THEY HIT ME.
I DON'T JUST SEE THE FUTURE. I EXPERIENCE IT.
MY WHOLE BODY EXPERIENCES DISASTERS AND IT'S--I'M WORRIED ABOUT IT GETTING TO ME.
AND I'M WORRIED ABOUT IT ALTERING YOUR ABILITY TO SEE YOUR VISIONS CLEARLY.
I DIDN'T EVEN THINK OF THAT.
BUT IF WE CAN FIGURE THIS ALL OUT...
...YOU MAY BE THE MOST IMPORTANT SUPER-POWERED PERSON TO COME ALONG SINCE--
AGH!
ULYSSES?
NNNAAGH!
WHAT IS IT?
TH-THANOS.
HIS NAME IS THANOS.
HE'S--HE'S COMING!

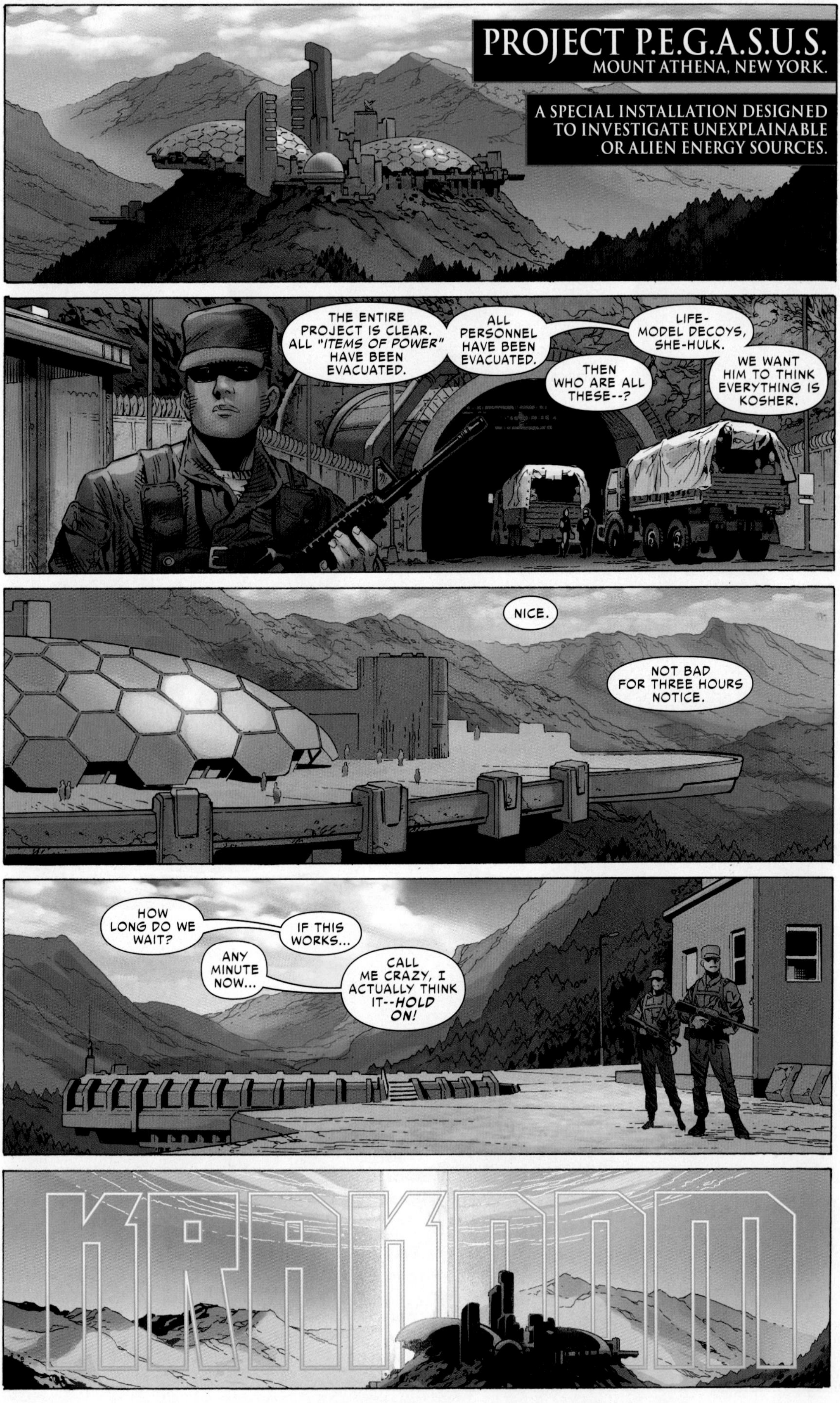
PROJECT P.E.G.A.S.U.S.
MOUNT ATHENA, NEW YORK.
A SPECIAL INSTALLATION DESIGNED TO INVESTIGATE UNEXPLAINABLE OR ALIEN ENERGY SOURCES.
THE ENTIRE PROJECT IS CLEAR. ALL "ITEMS OF POWER" HAVE BEEN EVACUATED.
ALL PERSONNEL HAVE BEEN EVACUATED.
LIFE-MODEL DECOYS, SHE-HULK.
THEN WHO ARE ALL THESE--?
WE WANT HIM TO THINK EVERYTHING IS KOSHER.
NICE.
NOT BAD FOR THREE HOURS NOTICE.
HOW LONG DO WE WAIT?
IF THIS WORKS...
ANY MINUTE NOW...
CALL ME CRAZY, I ACTUALLY THINK IT--HOLD ON!
KRAKOOM

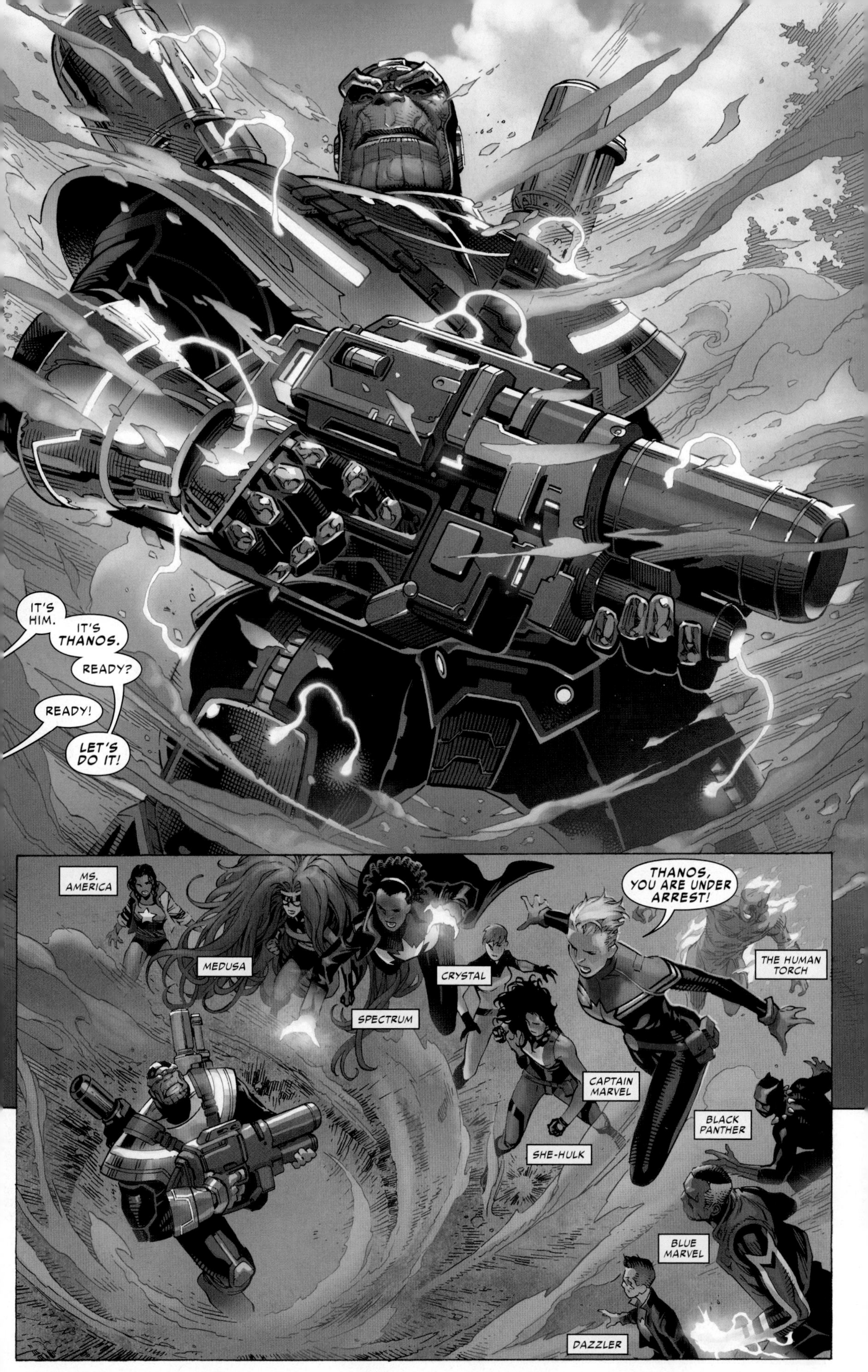
IT'S HIM.
IT'S THANOS.
READY?
READY!
LET'S DO IT!
MS. AMERICA
MEDUSA
SPECTRUM
CRYSTAL
THANOS, YOU ARE UNDER ARREST!
THE HUMAN TORCH
CAPTAIN MARVEL
SHE-HULK
BLACK PANTHER
BLUE MARVEL
DAZZLER

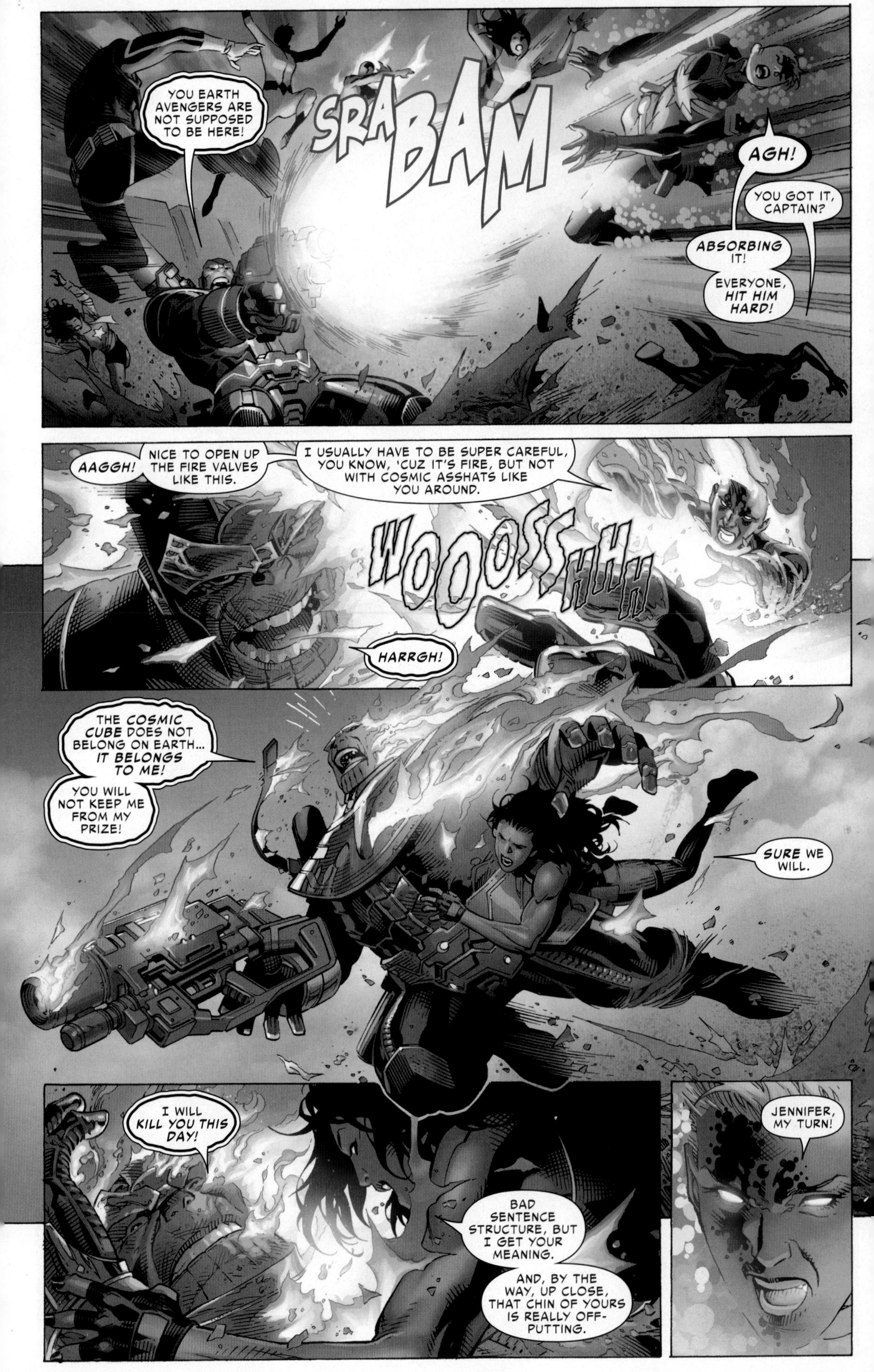
YOU EARTH AVENGERS ARE NOT SUPPOSED TO BE HERE!
SRABAM
AGH!
YOU GOT IT, CAPTAIN?
ABSORBING IT!
EVERYONE, HIT HIM HARD!
AAGGH!
NICE TO OPEN UP THE FIRE VALVES LIKE THIS.
I USUALLY HAVE TO BE SUPER CAREFUL, YOU KNOW, 'CUZ IT'S FIRE, BUT NOT WITH COSMIC ASSHATS LIKE YOU AROUND.
WOOOSSHHH
HARRGH!
THE COSMIC CUBE DOES NOT BELONG ON EARTH... IT BELONGS TO ME!
YOU WILL NOT KEEP ME FROM MY PRIZE!
SURE WE WILL.
I WILL KILL YOU THIS DAY!
BAD SENTENCE STRUCTURE, BUT I GET YOUR MEANING.
AND, BY THE WAY, UP CLOSE, THAT CHIN OF YOURS IS REALLY OFF-PUTTING.
JENNIFER, MY TURN!

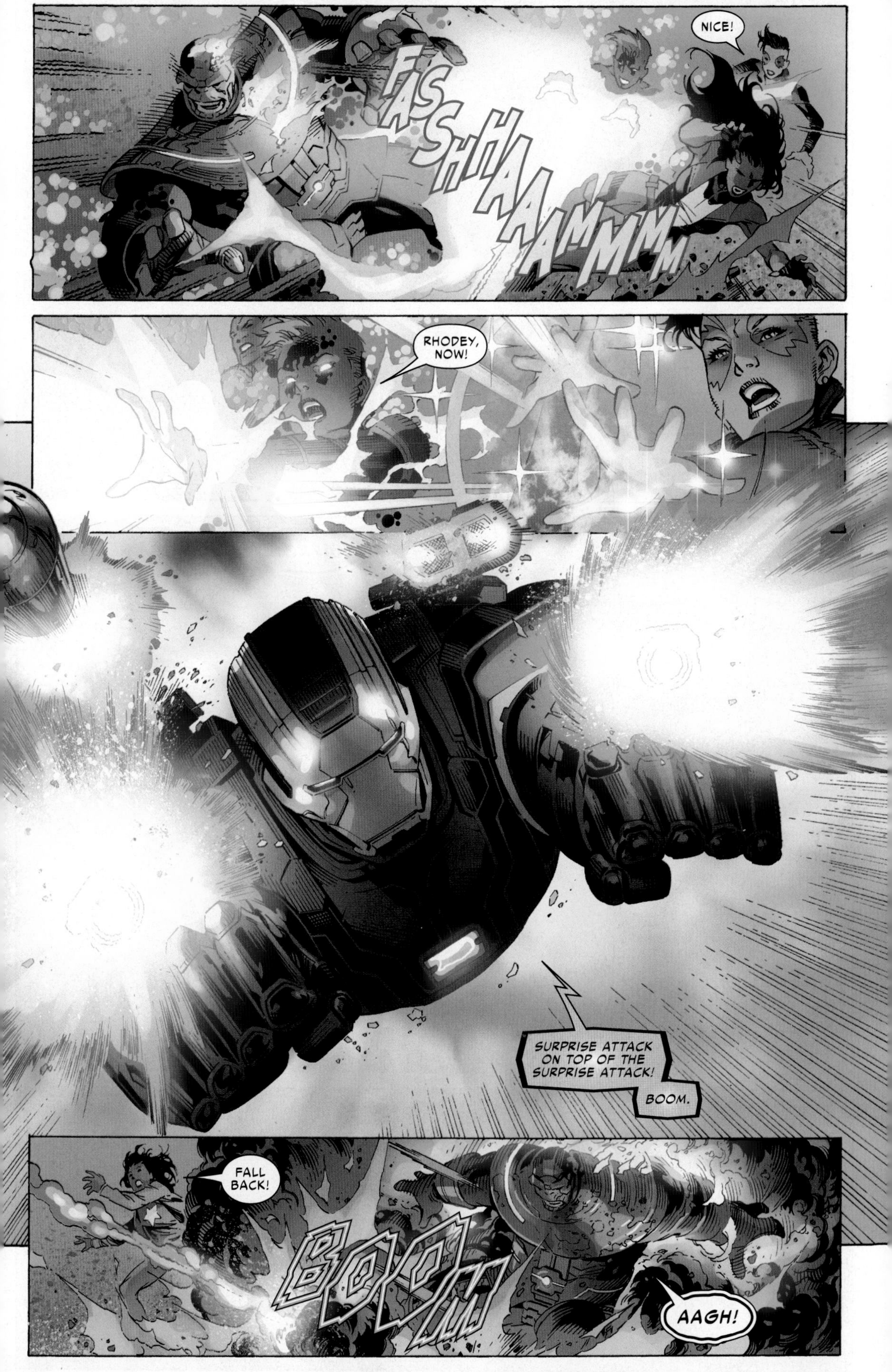
FASHHAAMMMM
NICE!
RHODEY, NOW!
SURPRISE ATTACK ON TOP OF THE SURPRISE ATTACK!
BOOM.
FALL BACK!
BOOOM
AAGH!

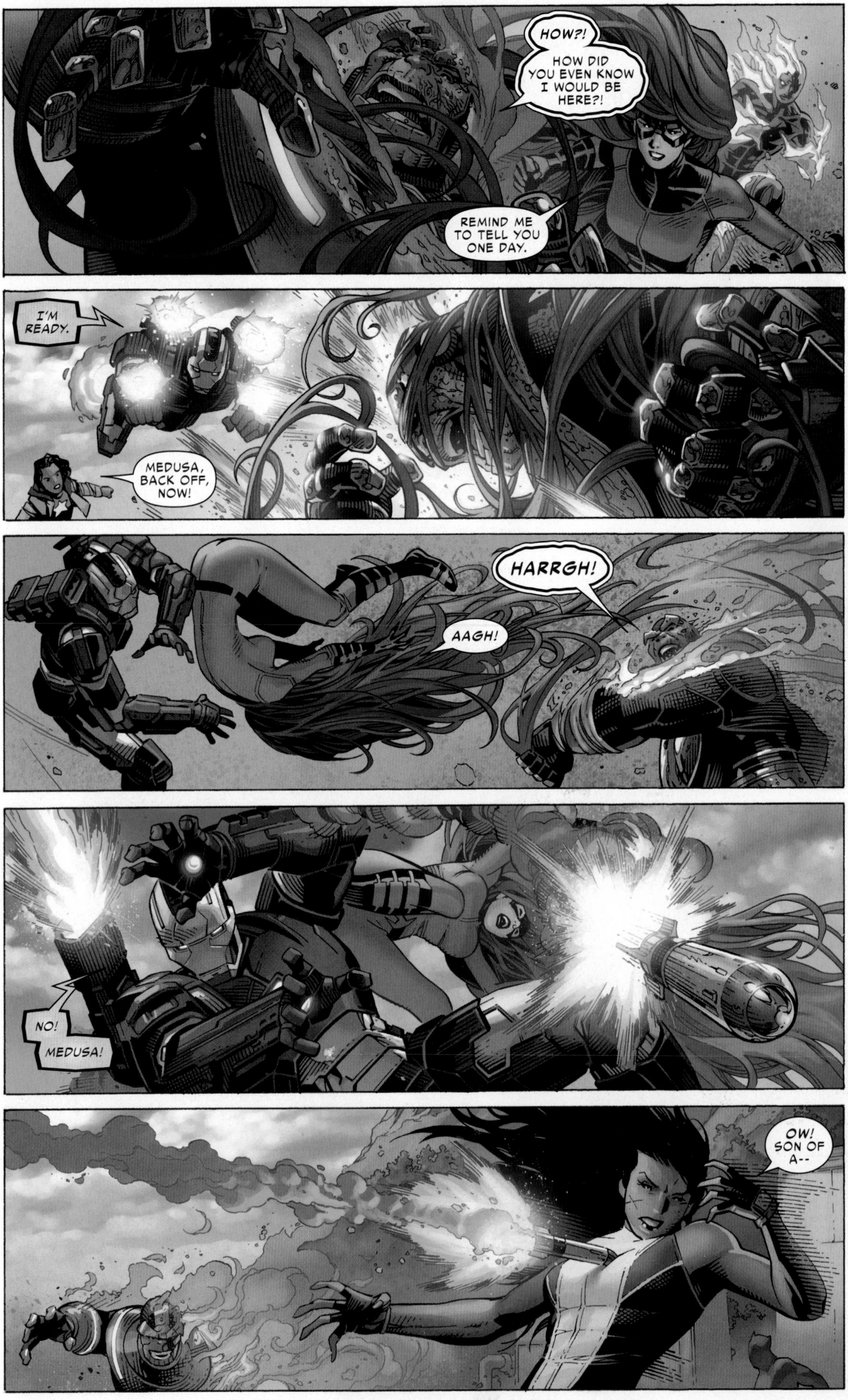
HOW?!
HOW DID YOU EVEN KNOW I WOULD BE HERE?!
REMIND ME TO TELL YOU ONE DAY.
I'M READY.
MEDUSA, BACK OFF, NOW!
HARRGH!
AAGH!
NO!
MEDUSA!
OW! SON OF A--

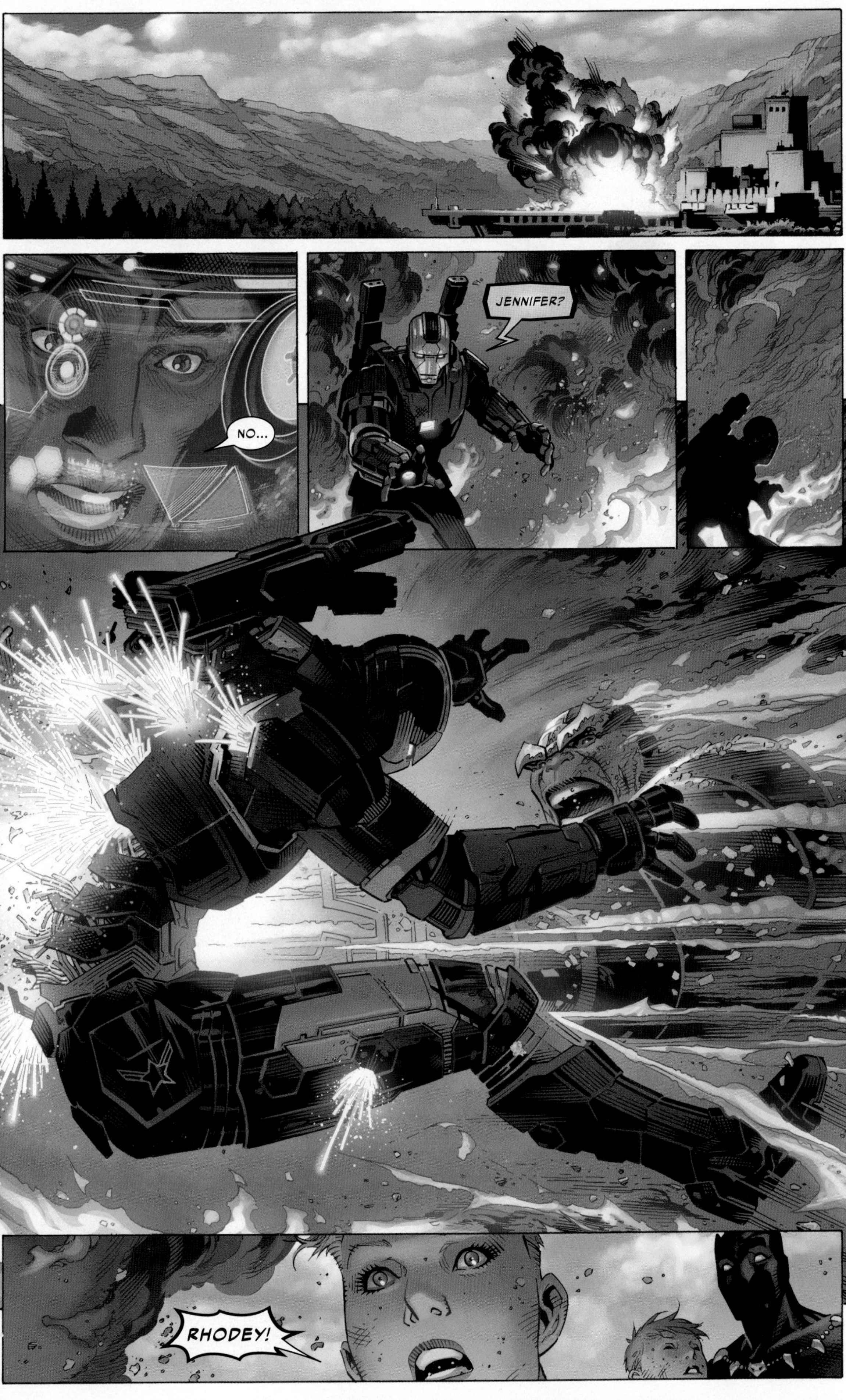
NO...
JENNIFER?
RHODEY!

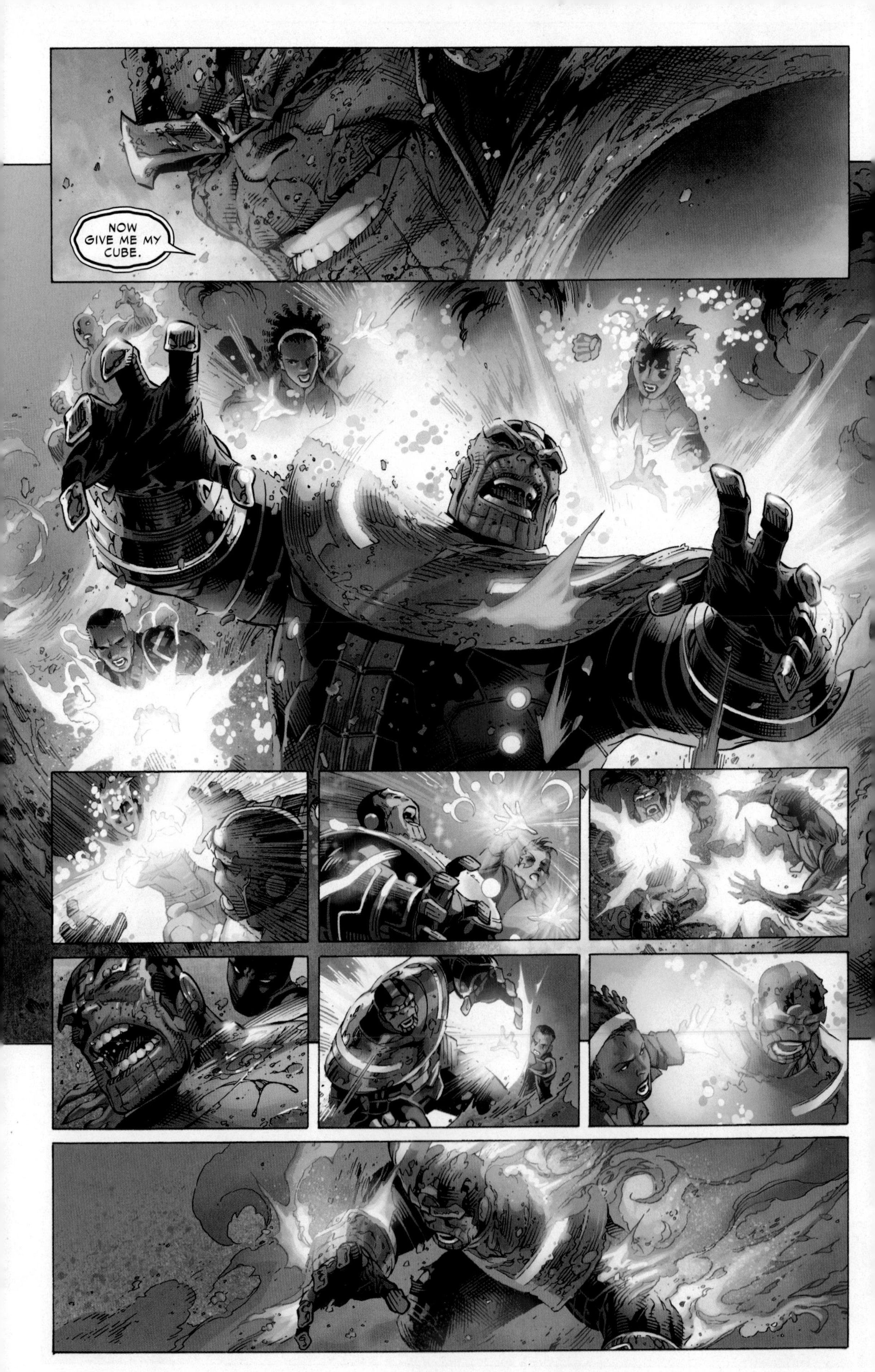
NOW GIVE ME MY CUBE.

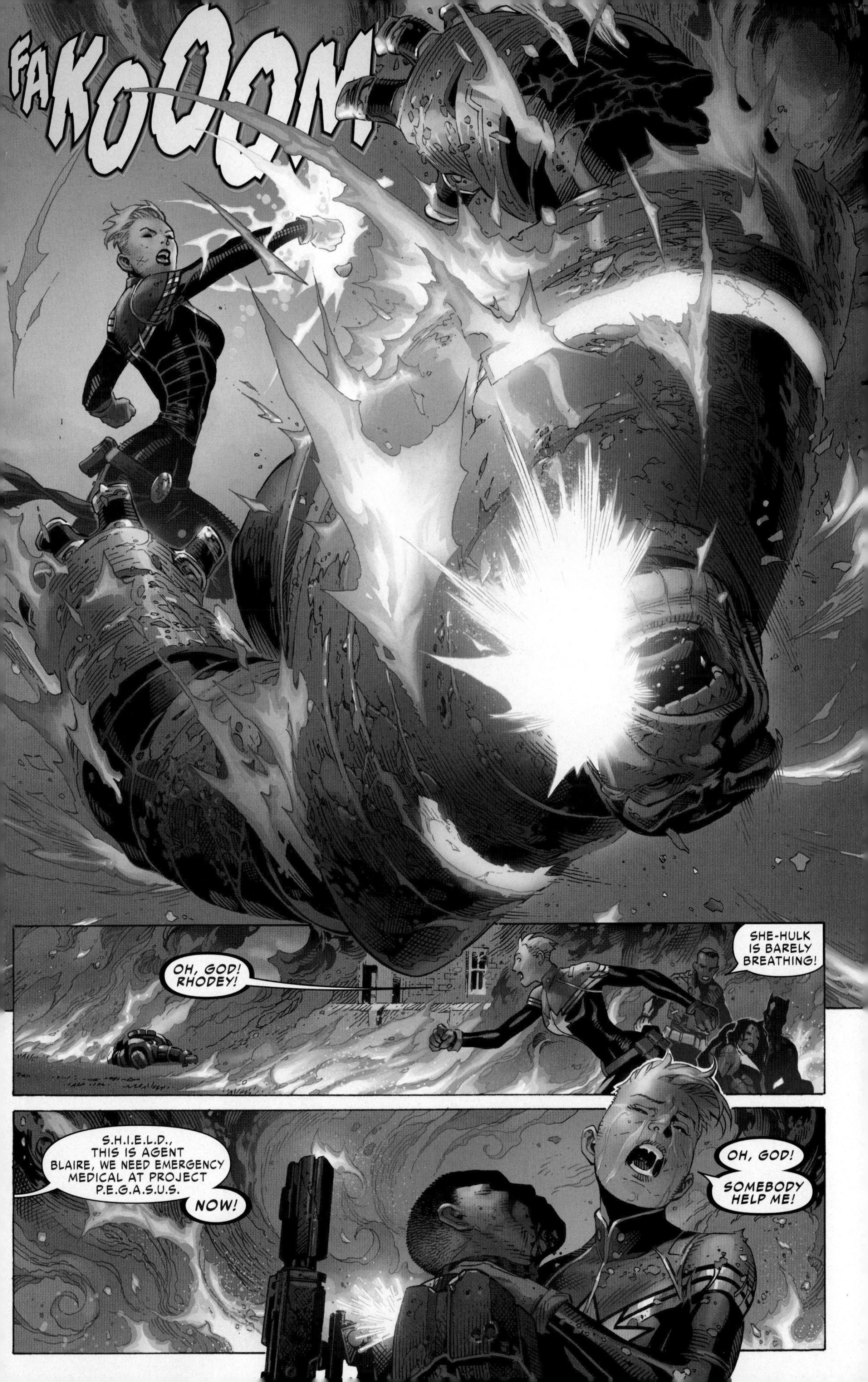
FAKOOOM
OH, GOD! RHODEY!
SHE-HULK IS BARELY BREATHING!
S.H.I.E.L.D., THIS IS AGENT BLAIRE, WE NEED EMERGENCY MEDICAL AT PROJECT P.E.G.A.S.U.S.
NOW!
OH, GOD!
SOMEBODY HELP ME!

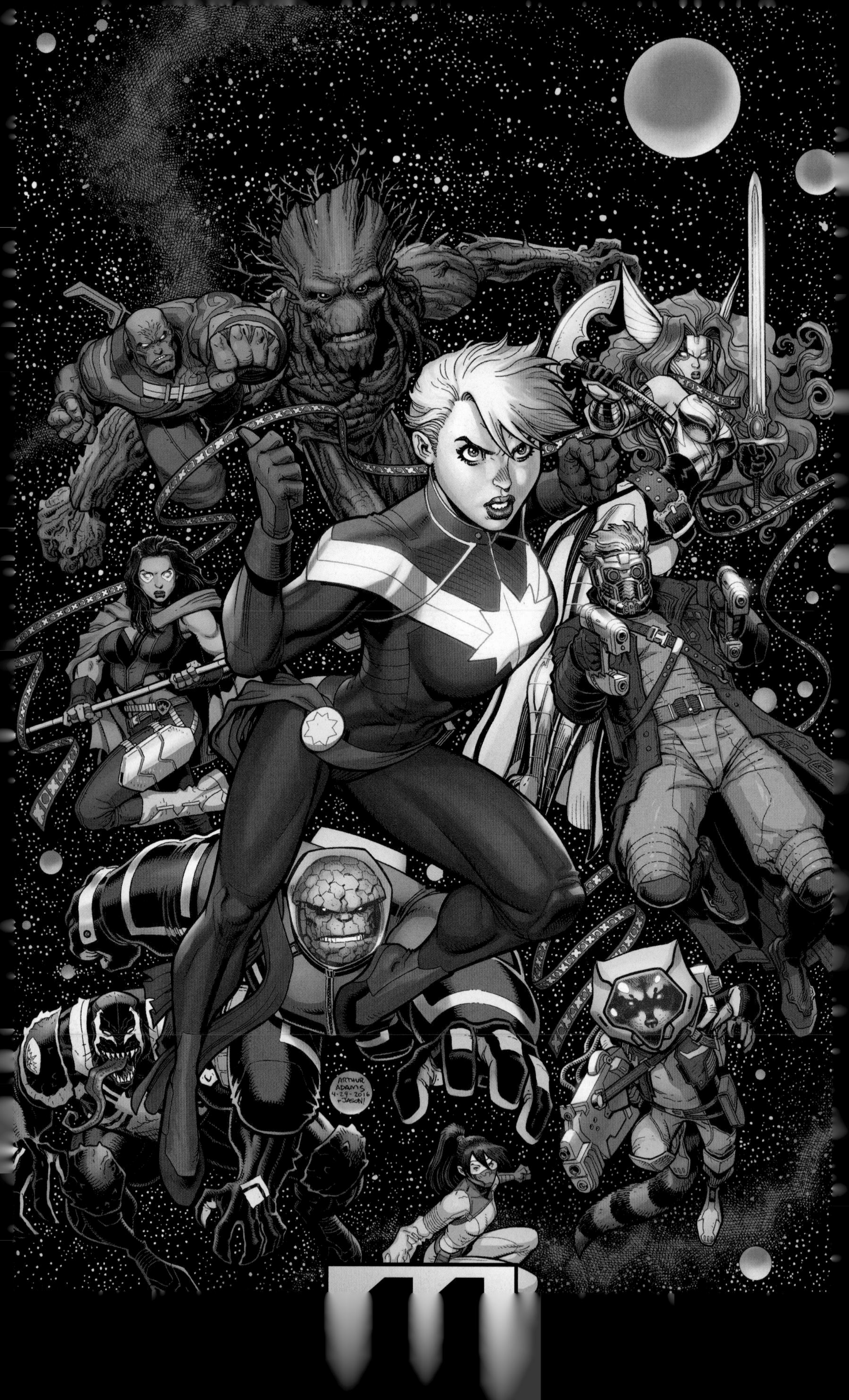
ARTHUR ADAMS 4-29-2016 +JASON!

CIVIL WAR II

GUARDIANS OF THE GALAXY

THE ENTIRE GALAXY IS A MESS. WARRING EMPIRES AND COSMIC TERRORISTS PLAGUE EVERY CORNER. SOMEONE HAS TO RISE ABOVE IT ALL AND FIGHT FOR THOSE WHO HAVE NO ONE TO FIGHT FOR THEM. A GROUP OF MISFITS — **DRAX THE DESTROYER**, **GAMORA**, **ROCKET RACCOON**, **GROOT**, **FLASH THOMPSON**, A.K.A. **VENOM**, **KITTY PRYDE**, AND **BEN GRIMM**, A.K.A. **THE THING** — JOINED TOGETHER UNDER THE LEADERSHIP OF **PETER QUILL**, A.K.A. **STAR-LORD**. THEY SERVE A HIGHER CAUSE AS THE **GUARDIANS OF THE GALAXY**.

THE GUARDIANS HAVE OVERTHROWN A PRISON PLANET, RESCUING INNOCENT POLITICAL SLAVES OF THE BADOON EMPIRE. ONE WAS THEIR OLD TEAMMATE ANGELA, WHO REJOINED THE GUARDIANS JUST AS CAPTAIN MARVEL, ANOTHER OLD TEAMMATE, CALLED TO ASK THEM TO RETURN TO EARTH.

THANKS TO AN INHUMAN WHO SEEMS TO BE ABLE TO PREDICT THE FUTURE, EARTH'S HEROES PREVENTED A CATACLYSMIC EVENT. CAPTAIN MARVEL BELIEVES THAT ACTING ON HIS VISIONS SAVES LIVES, BUT THERE HAVE BEEN TERRIBLE COSTS. A NEW SUPER HERO CIVIL WAR IS IMMINENT. NOW THE GUARDIANS WILL HAVE TO MAKE A CHOICE: PROTECT THE FUTURE...OR CHANGE IT?

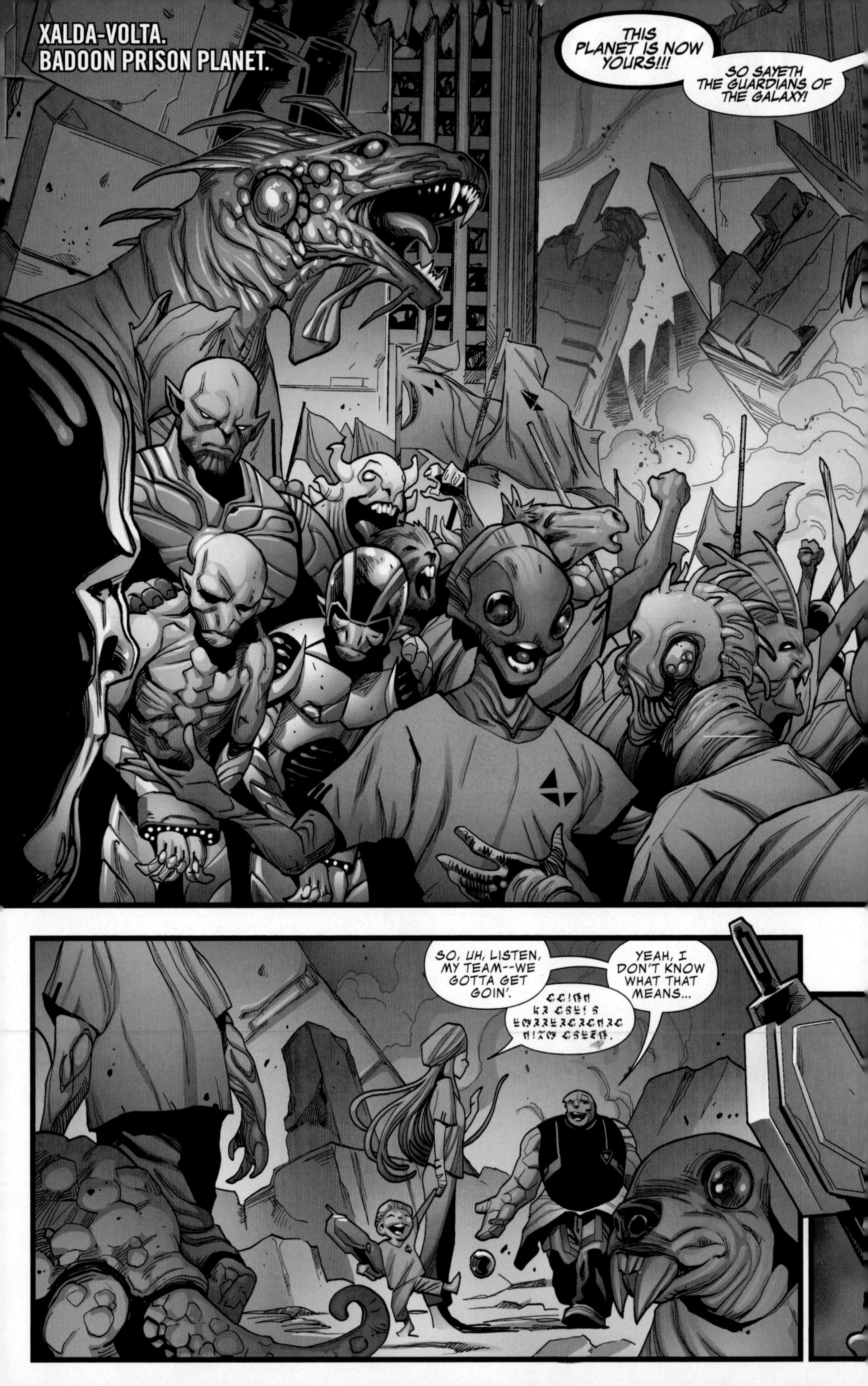
XALDA-VOLTA.
BADOON PRISON PLANET.
THIS PLANET IS NOW YOURS!!!
SO SAYETH THE GUARDIANS OF THE GALAXY!
SO, UH, LISTEN, MY TEAM--WE GOTTA GET GOIN'.
YEAH, I DON'T KNOW WHAT THAT MEANS...

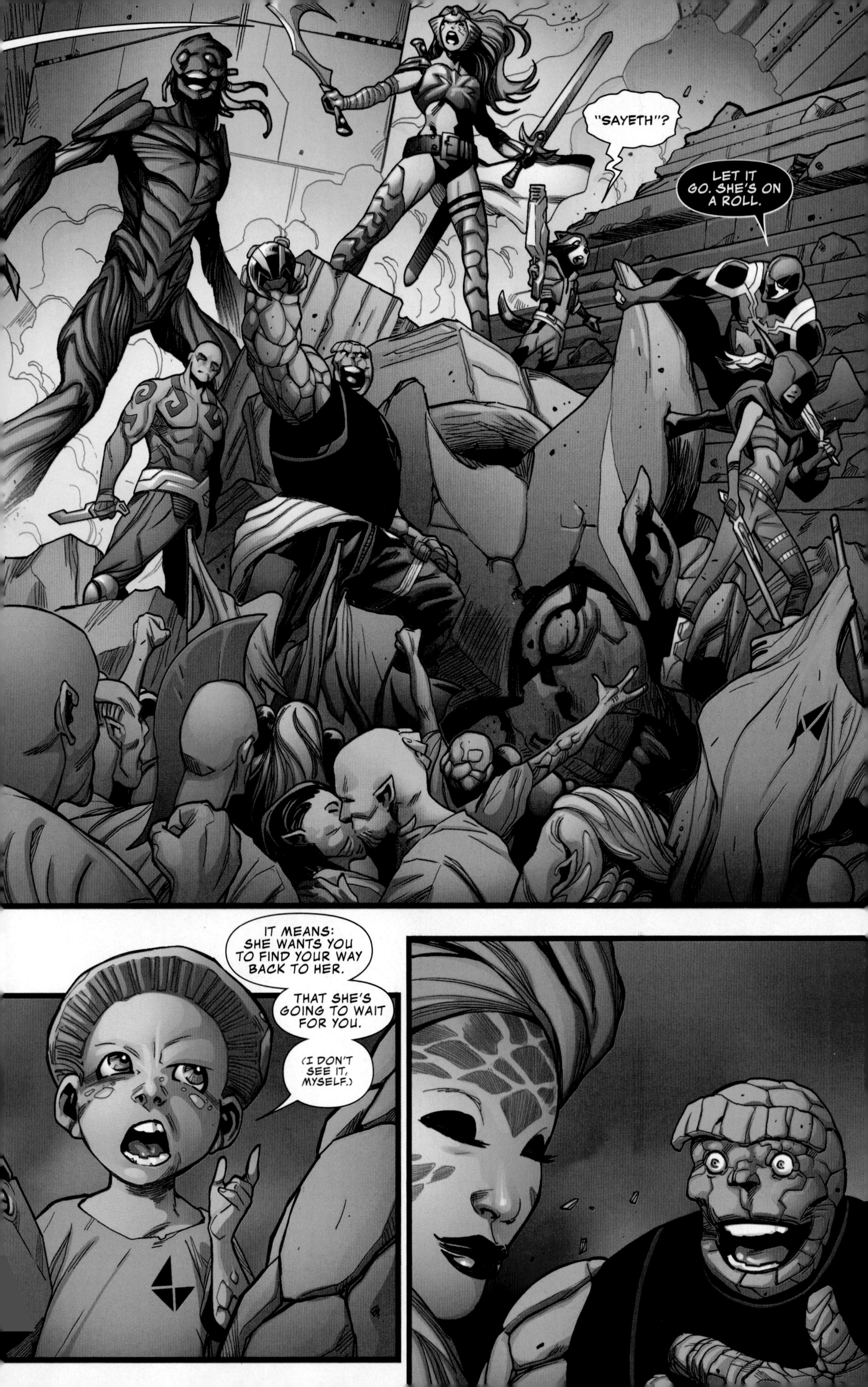
"SAYETH"?
LET IT GO. SHE'S ON A ROLL.
IT MEANS: SHE WANTS YOU TO FIND YOUR WAY BACK TO HER.
THAT SHE'S GOING TO WAIT FOR YOU.
(I DON'T SEE IT, MYSELF.)

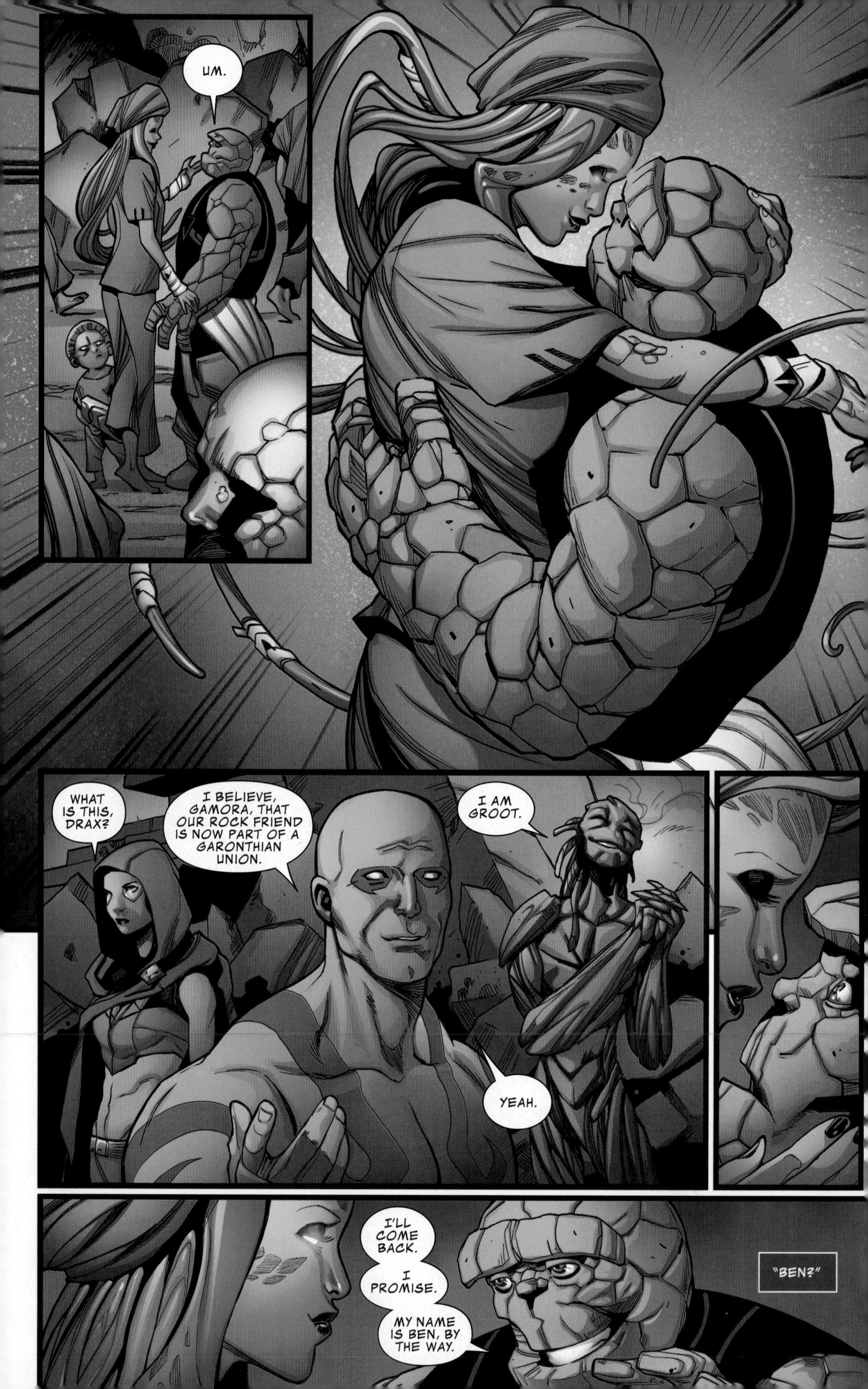
UM.
WHAT IS THIS, DRAX?
I BELIEVE, GAMORA, THAT OUR ROCK FRIEND IS NOW PART OF A GARONTHIAN UNION.
I AM GROOT.
YEAH.
I'LL COME BACK.
I PROMISE.
MY NAME IS BEN, BY THE WAY.
"BEN?"

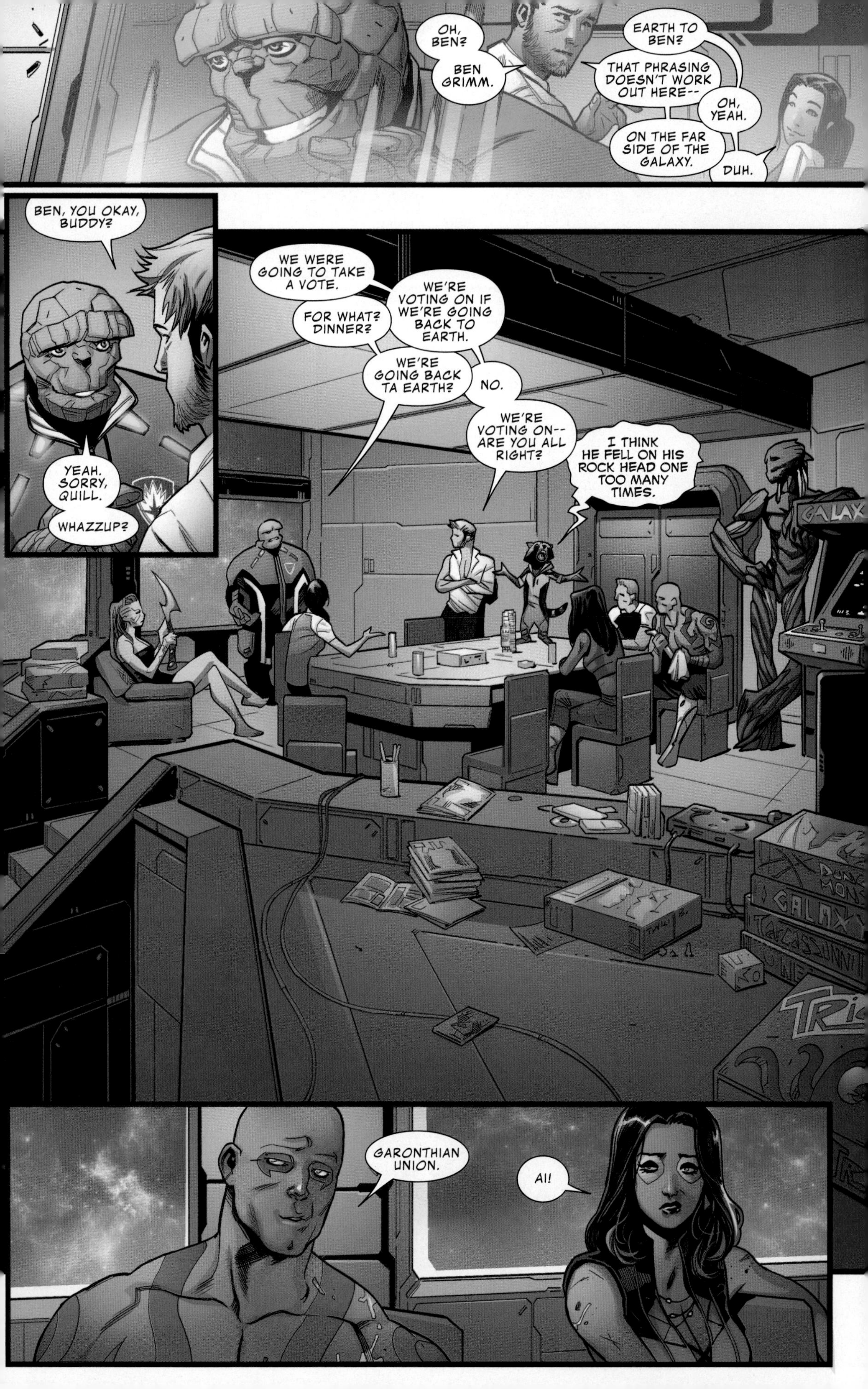
OH, BEN?
BEN GRIMM.
EARTH TO BEN?
THAT PHRASING DOESN'T WORK OUT HERE--
ON THE FAR SIDE OF THE GALAXY.
OH, YEAH.
DUH.
BEN, YOU OKAY, BUDDY?
YEAH. SORRY, QUILL.
WHAZZUP?
WE WERE GOING TO TAKE A VOTE.
FOR WHAT? DINNER?
WE'RE VOTING ON IF WE'RE GOING BACK TO EARTH.
WE'RE GOING BACK TA EARTH?
NO.
WE'RE VOTING ON-- ARE YOU ALL RIGHT?
I THINK HE FELL ON HIS ROCK HEAD ONE TOO MANY TIMES.
GARONTHIAN UNION.
AI!

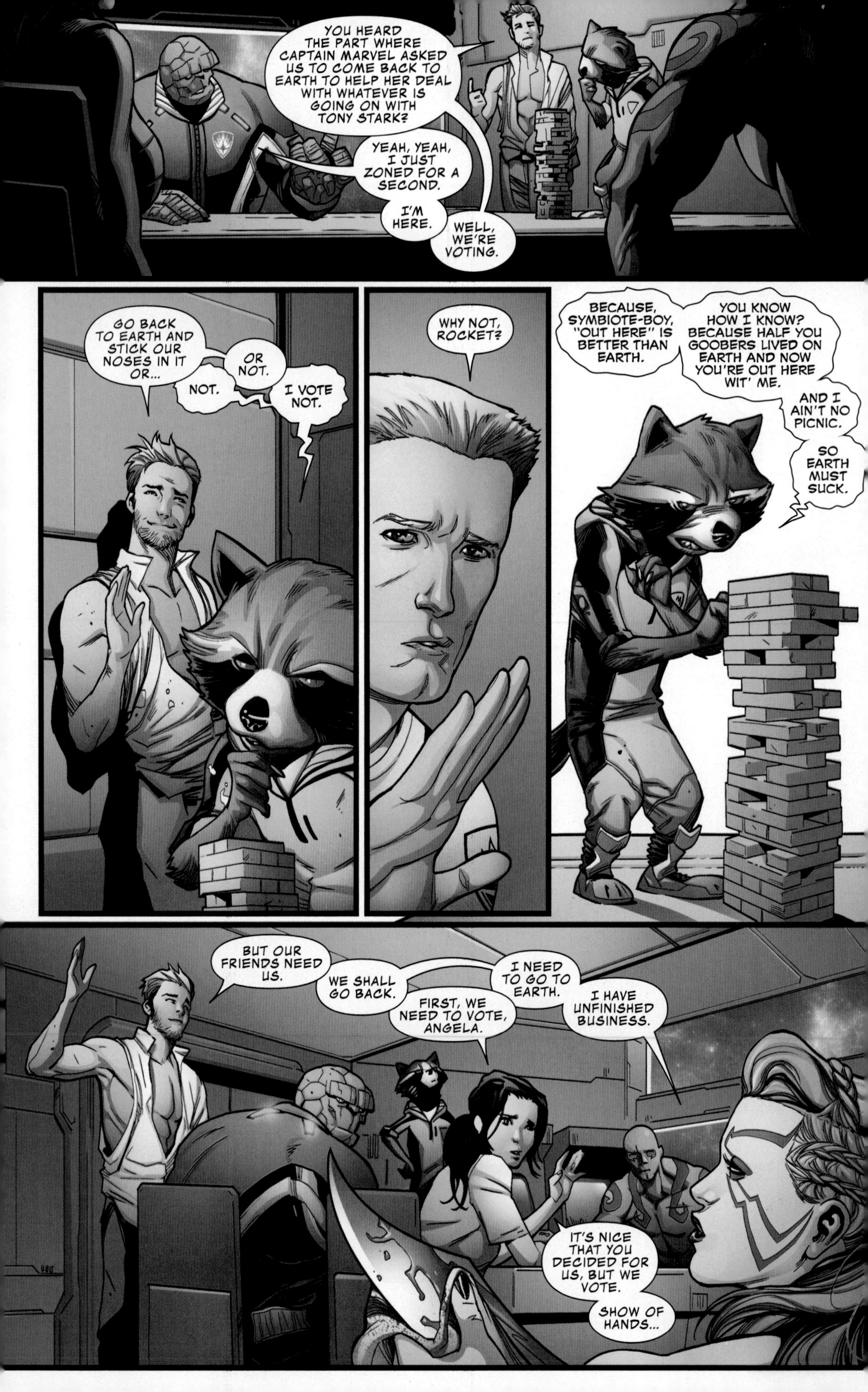
YOU HEARD THE PART WHERE CAPTAIN MARVEL ASKED US TO COME BACK TO EARTH TO HELP HER DEAL WITH WHATEVER IS GOING ON WITH TONY STARK?
YEAH, YEAH, I JUST ZONED FOR A SECOND.
I'M HERE.
WELL, WE'RE VOTING.
GO BACK TO EARTH AND STICK OUR NOSES IN IT OR...
NOT.
OR NOT.
I VOTE NOT.
WHY NOT, ROCKET?
BECAUSE, SYMBIOTE-BOY, "OUT HERE" IS BETTER THAN EARTH.
YOU KNOW HOW I KNOW? BECAUSE HALF YOU GOOBERS LIVED ON EARTH AND NOW YOU'RE OUT HERE WIT' ME.
AND I AIN'T NO PICNIC.
SO EARTH MUST SUCK.
BUT OUR FRIENDS NEED US.
WE SHALL GO BACK.
I NEED TO GO TO EARTH.
FIRST, WE NEED TO VOTE, ANGELA.
I HAVE UNFINISHED BUSINESS.
IT'S NICE THAT YOU DECIDED FOR US, BUT WE VOTE.
SHOW OF HANDS...

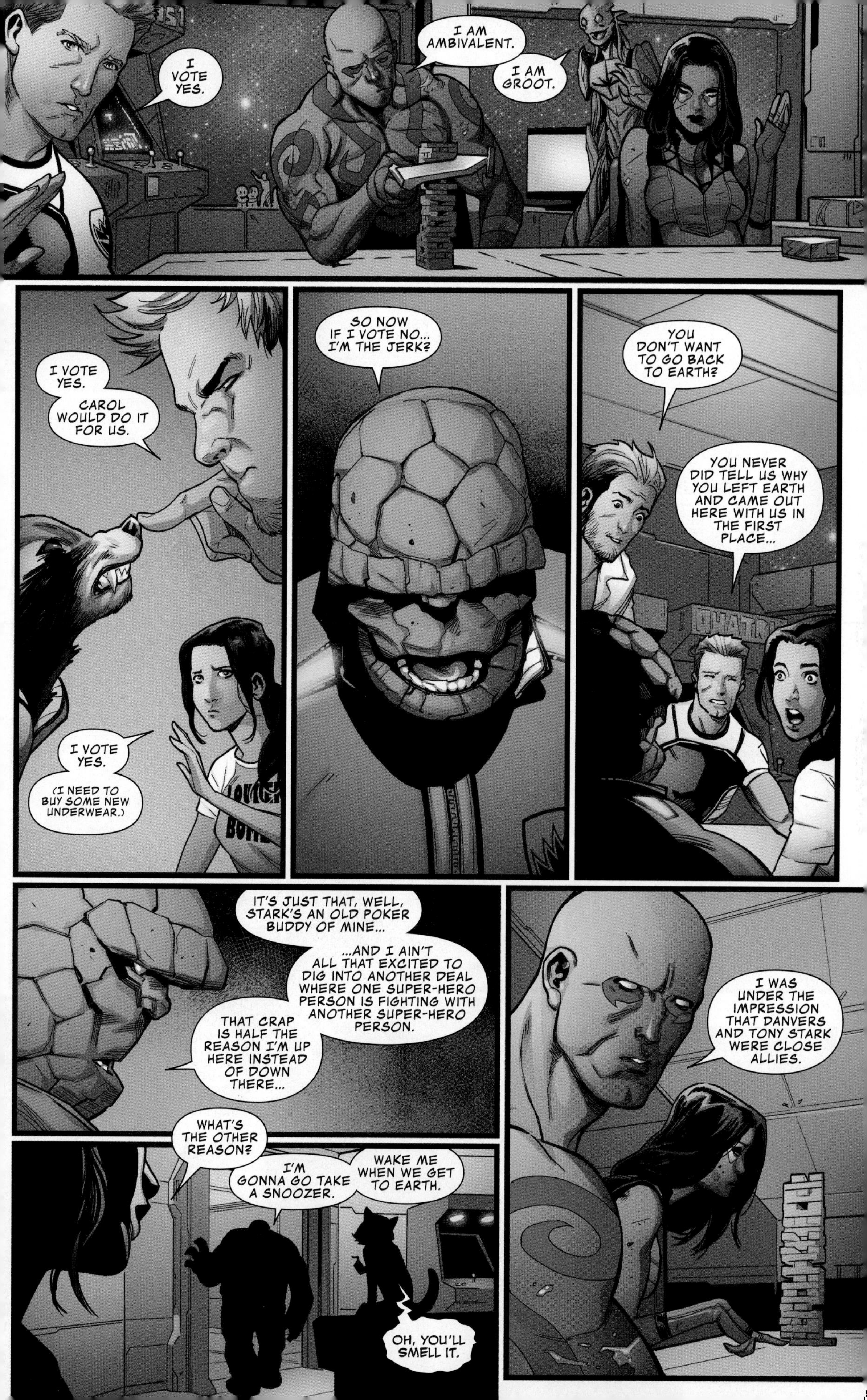
I VOTE YES.
I AM AMBIVALENT.
I AM GROOT.
I VOTE YES.
CAROL WOULD DO IT FOR US.
I VOTE YES.
(I NEED TO BUY SOME NEW UNDERWEAR.)
SO NOW IF I VOTE NO... I'M THE JERK?
YOU DON'T WANT TO GO BACK TO EARTH?
YOU NEVER DID TELL US WHY YOU LEFT EARTH AND CAME OUT HERE WITH US IN THE FIRST PLACE...
IT'S JUST THAT, WELL, STARK'S AN OLD POKER BUDDY OF MINE...
...AND I AIN'T ALL THAT EXCITED TO DIG INTO ANOTHER DEAL WHERE ONE SUPER-HERO PERSON IS FIGHTING WITH ANOTHER SUPER-HERO PERSON.
THAT CRAP IS HALF THE REASON I'M UP HERE INSTEAD OF DOWN THERE...
I WAS UNDER THE IMPRESSION THAT DANVERS AND TONY STARK WERE CLOSE ALLIES.
WHAT'S THE OTHER REASON?
I'M GONNA GO TAKE A SNOOZER.
WAKE ME WHEN WE GET TO EARTH.
OH, YOU'LL SMELL IT.

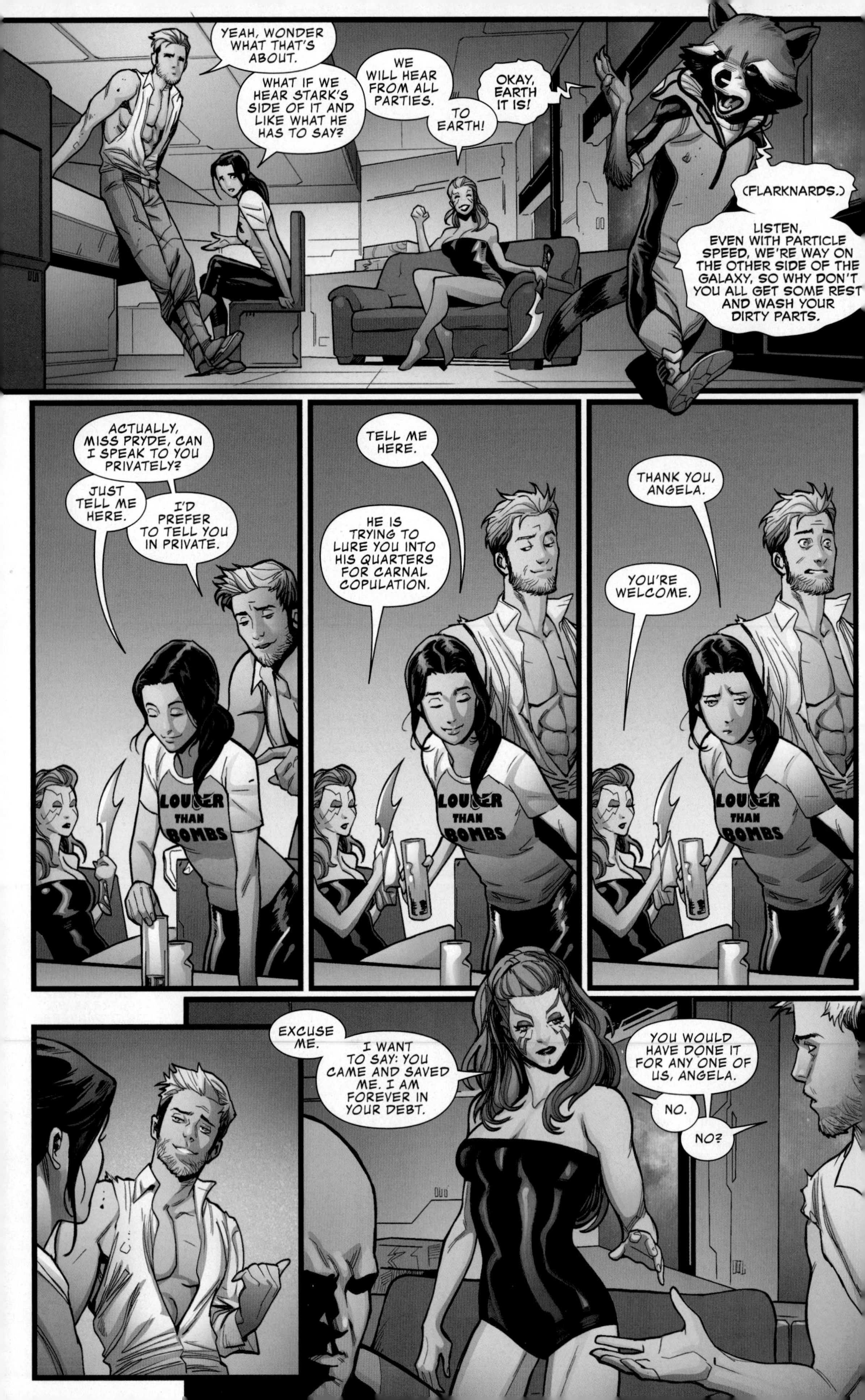
YEAH, WONDER WHAT THAT'S ABOUT.
WHAT IF WE HEAR STARK'S SIDE OF IT AND LIKE WHAT HE HAS TO SAY?
WE WILL HEAR FROM ALL PARTIES.
TO EARTH!
OKAY, EARTH IT IS!
(FLARKNARDS.)
LISTEN, EVEN WITH PARTICLE SPEED, WE'RE WAY ON THE OTHER SIDE OF THE GALAXY, SO WHY DON'T YOU ALL GET SOME REST AND WASH YOUR DIRTY PARTS.
ACTUALLY, MISS PRYDE, CAN I SPEAK TO YOU PRIVATELY?
JUST TELL ME HERE.
I'D PREFER TO TELL YOU IN PRIVATE.
LOUDER THAN BOMBS
TELL ME HERE.
HE IS TRYING TO LURE YOU INTO HIS QUARTERS FOR CARNAL COPULATION.
THANK YOU, ANGELA.
YOU'RE WELCOME.
EXCUSE ME.
I WANT TO SAY: YOU CAME AND SAVED ME. I AM FOREVER IN YOUR DEBT.
YOU WOULD HAVE DONE IT FOR ANY ONE OF US, ANGELA.
NO.
NO?

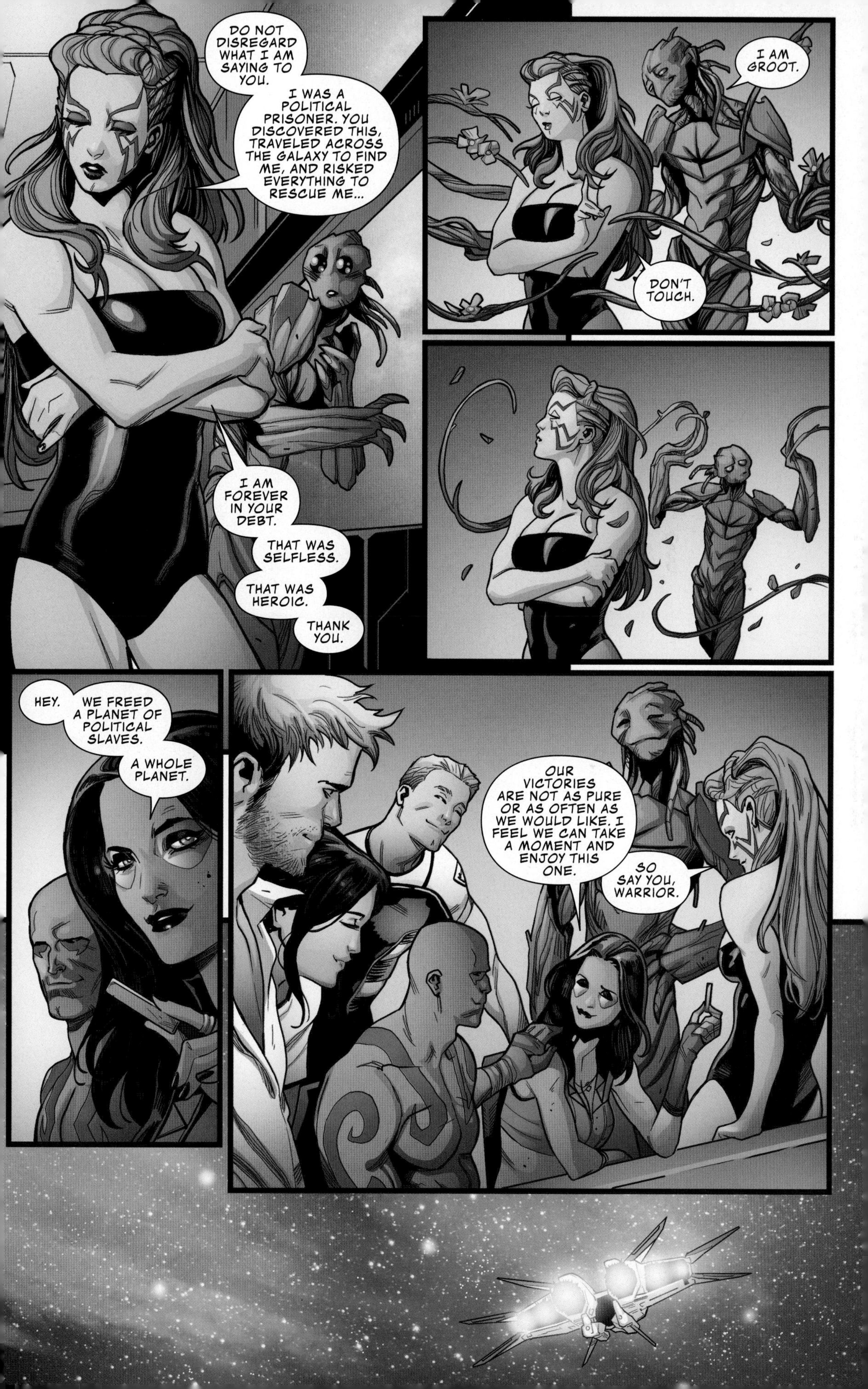

DO NOT DISREGARD WHAT I AM SAYING TO YOU.
I WAS A POLITICAL PRISONER. YOU DISCOVERED THIS, TRAVELED ACROSS THE GALAXY TO FIND ME, AND RISKED EVERYTHING TO RESCUE ME...
I AM FOREVER IN YOUR DEBT.
THAT WAS SELFLESS.
THAT WAS HEROIC.
THANK YOU.
I AM GROOT.
DON'T TOUCH.
HEY.
WE FREED A PLANET OF POLITICAL SLAVES.
A WHOLE PLANET.
OUR VICTORIES ARE NOT AS PURE OR AS OFTEN AS WE WOULD LIKE. I FEEL WE CAN TAKE A MOMENT AND ENJOY THIS ONE.
SO SAY YOU, WARRIOR.

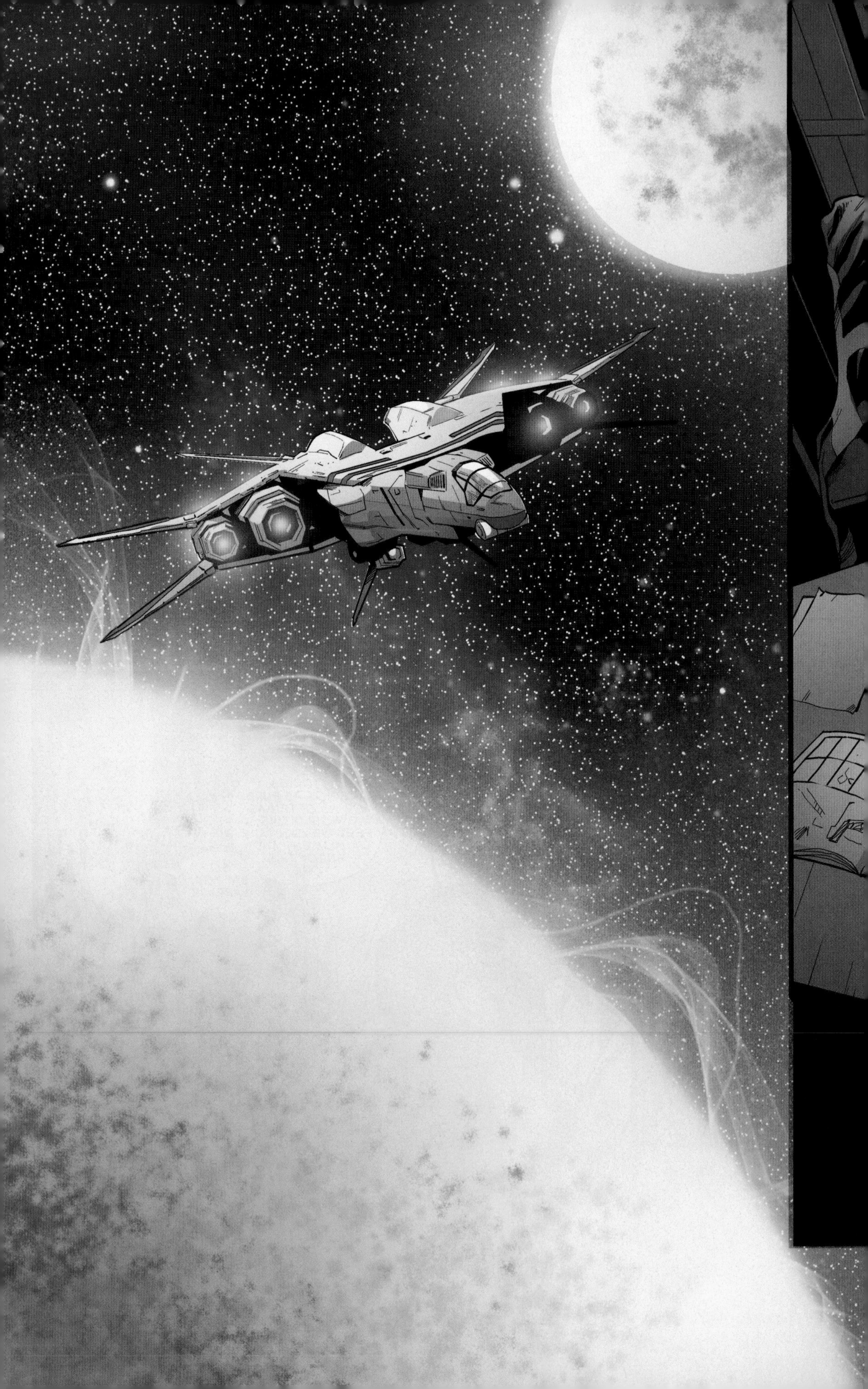

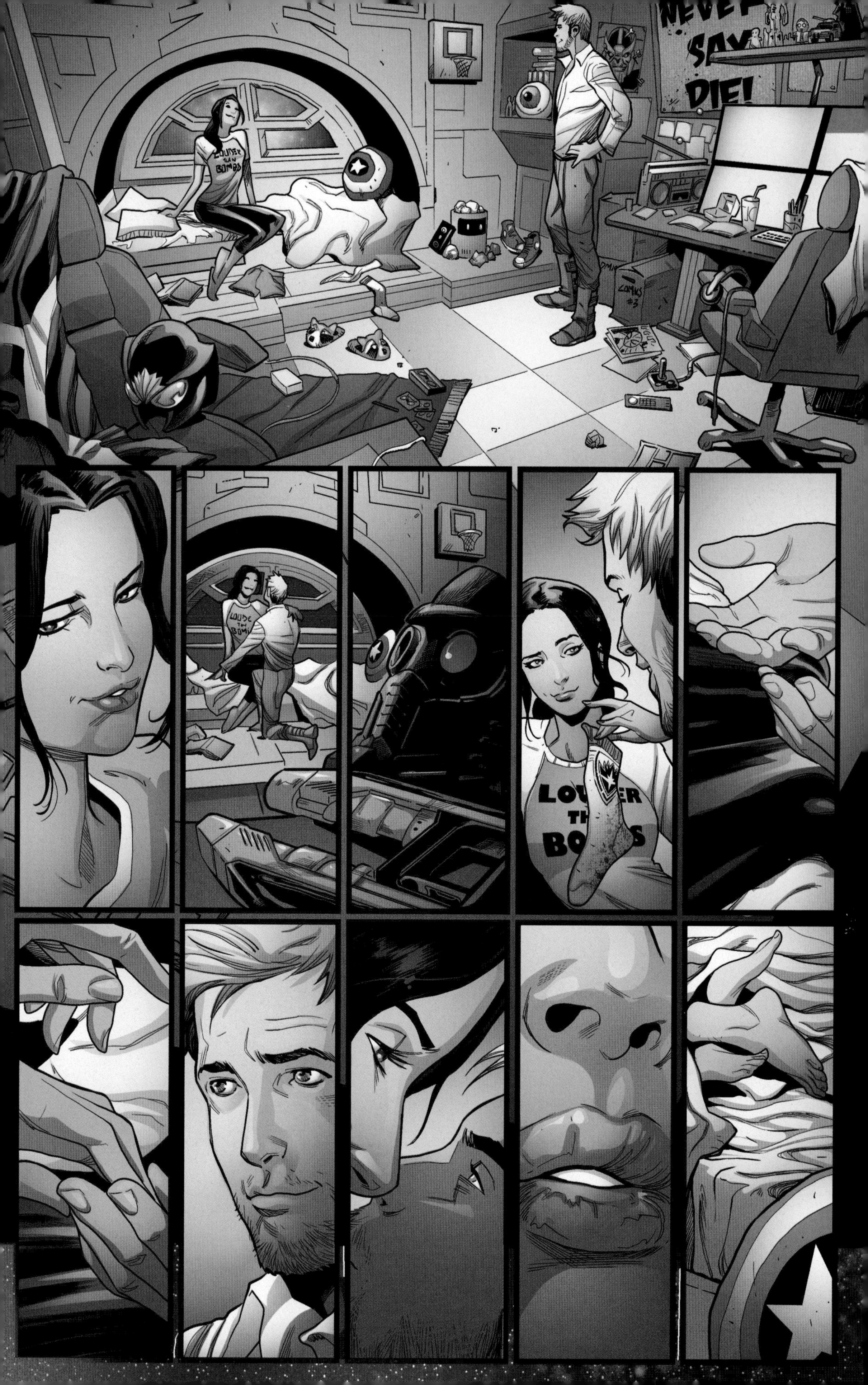
SAY DIE!
LOUDER THAN BOMBS

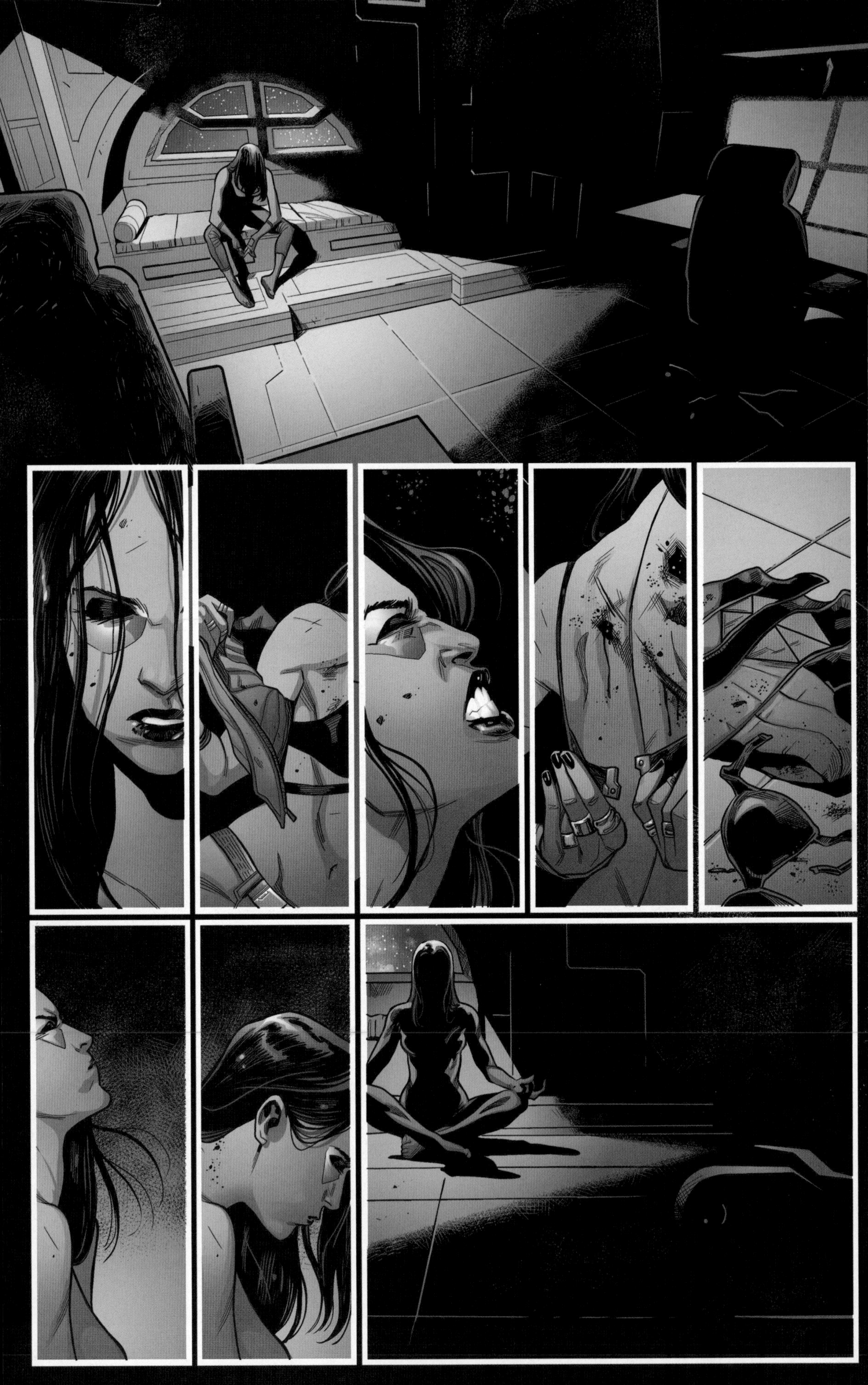

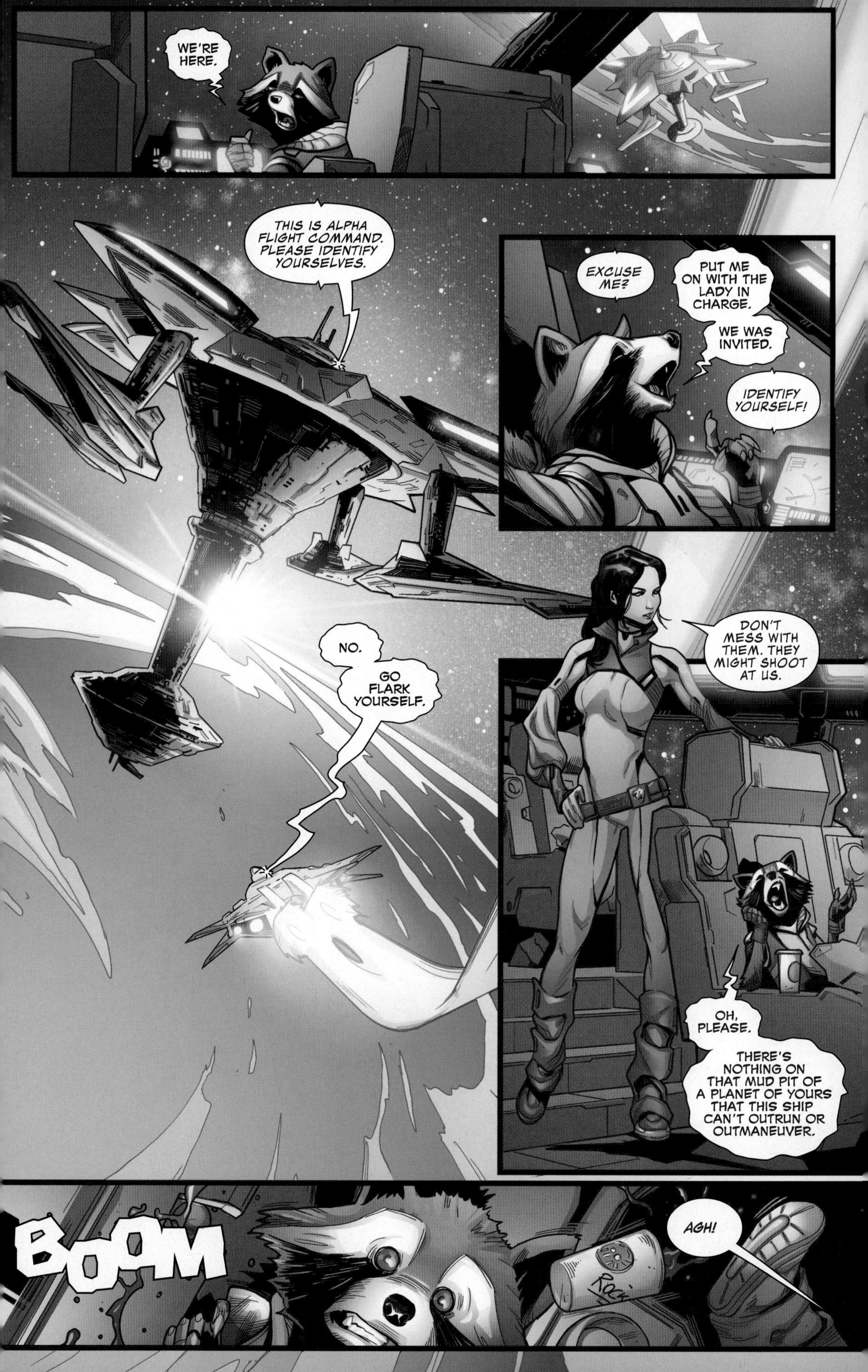
WE'RE HERE.
THIS IS ALPHA FLIGHT COMMAND. PLEASE IDENTIFY YOURSELVES.
EXCUSE ME?
PUT ME ON WITH THE LADY IN CHARGE.
WE WAS INVITED.
IDENTIFY YOURSELF!
NO.
GO FLARK YOURSELF.
DON'T MESS WITH THEM. THEY MIGHT SHOOT AT US.
OH, PLEASE.
THERE'S NOTHING ON THAT MUD PIT OF A PLANET OF YOURS THAT THIS SHIP CAN'T OUTRUN OR OUTMANEUVER.
BOOM
AGH!

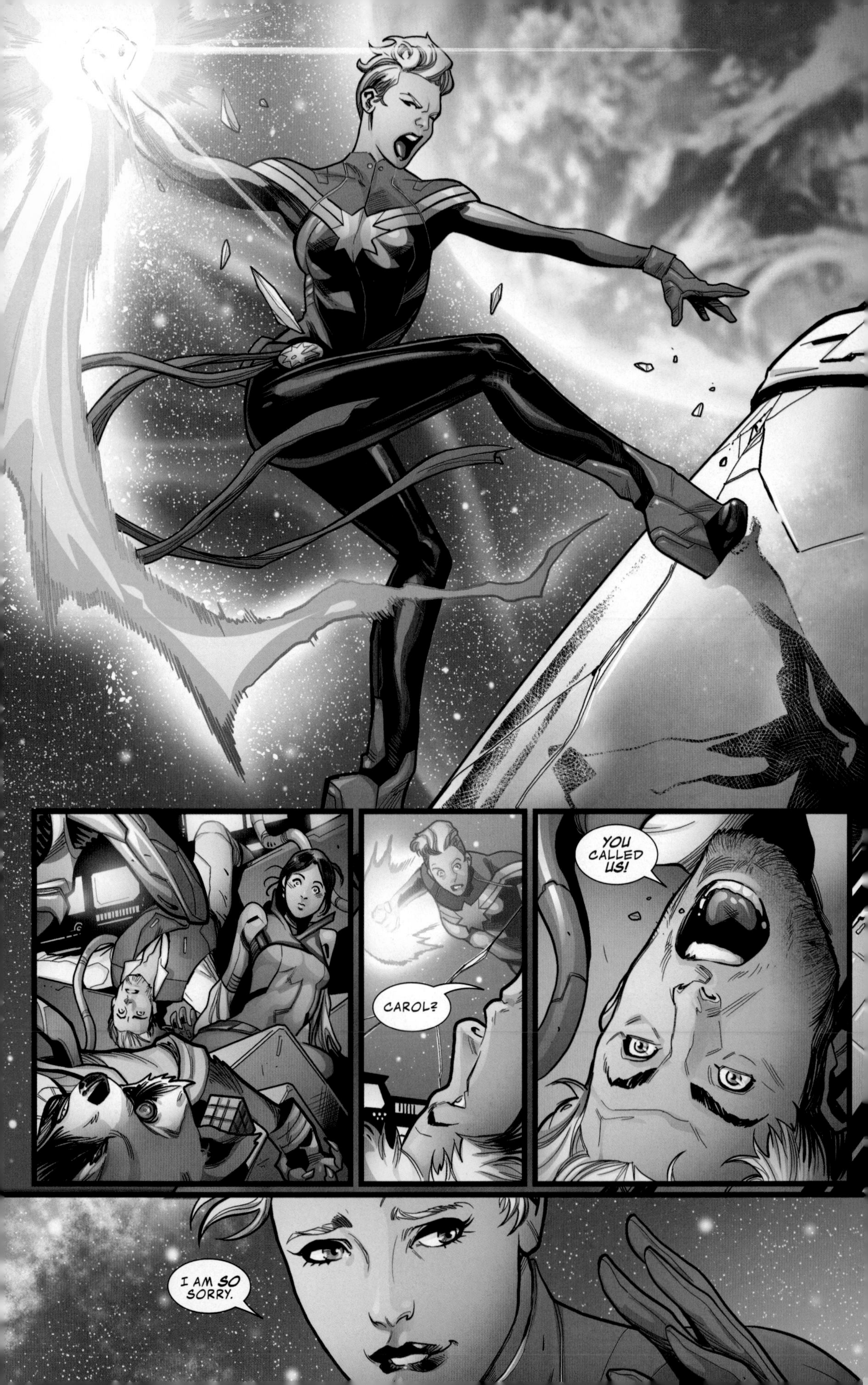
CAROL?
YOU CALLED US!
I AM SO SORRY.

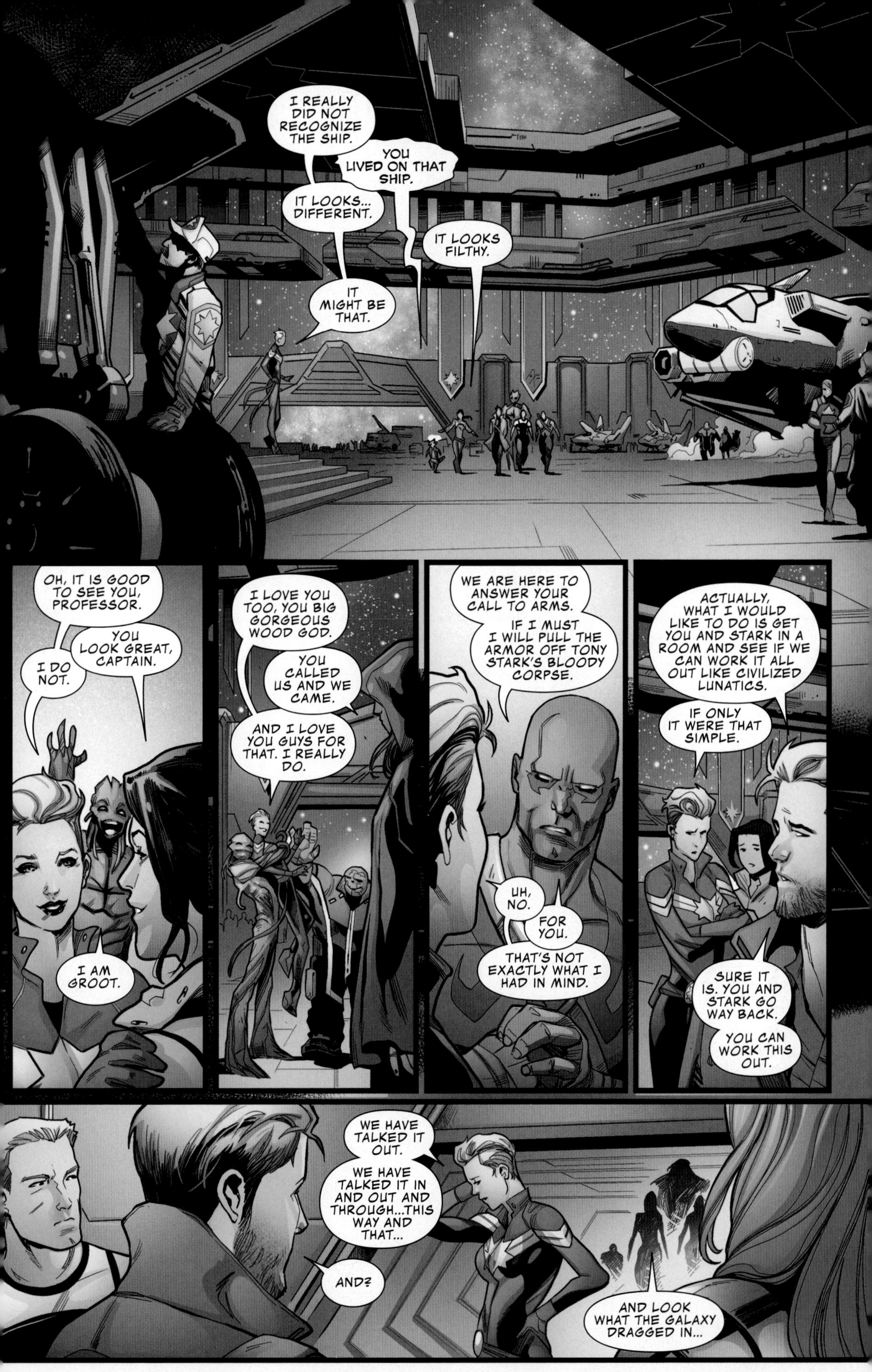

I REALLY DID NOT RECOGNIZE THE SHIP.
YOU LIVED ON THAT SHIP.
IT LOOKS... DIFFERENT.
IT LOOKS FILTHY.
IT MIGHT BE THAT.
OH, IT IS GOOD TO SEE YOU, PROFESSOR.
YOU LOOK GREAT, CAPTAIN.
I DO NOT.
I AM GROOT.
I LOVE YOU TOO, YOU BIG GORGEOUS WOOD GOD.
YOU CALLED US AND WE CAME.
AND I LOVE YOU GUYS FOR THAT. I REALLY DO.
WE ARE HERE TO ANSWER YOUR CALL TO ARMS.
IF I MUST I WILL PULL THE ARMOR OFF TONY STARK'S BLOODY CORPSE.
UH, NO.
FOR YOU.
THAT'S NOT EXACTLY WHAT I HAD IN MIND.
ACTUALLY, WHAT I WOULD LIKE TO DO IS GET YOU AND STARK IN A ROOM AND SEE IF WE CAN WORK IT ALL OUT LIKE CIVILIZED LUNATICS.
IF ONLY IT WERE THAT SIMPLE.
SURE IT IS. YOU AND STARK GO WAY BACK.
YOU CAN WORK THIS OUT.
WE HAVE TALKED IT OUT.
WE HAVE TALKED IT IN AND OUT AND THROUGH...THIS WAY AND THAT...
AND?
AND LOOK WHAT THE GALAXY DRAGGED IN...

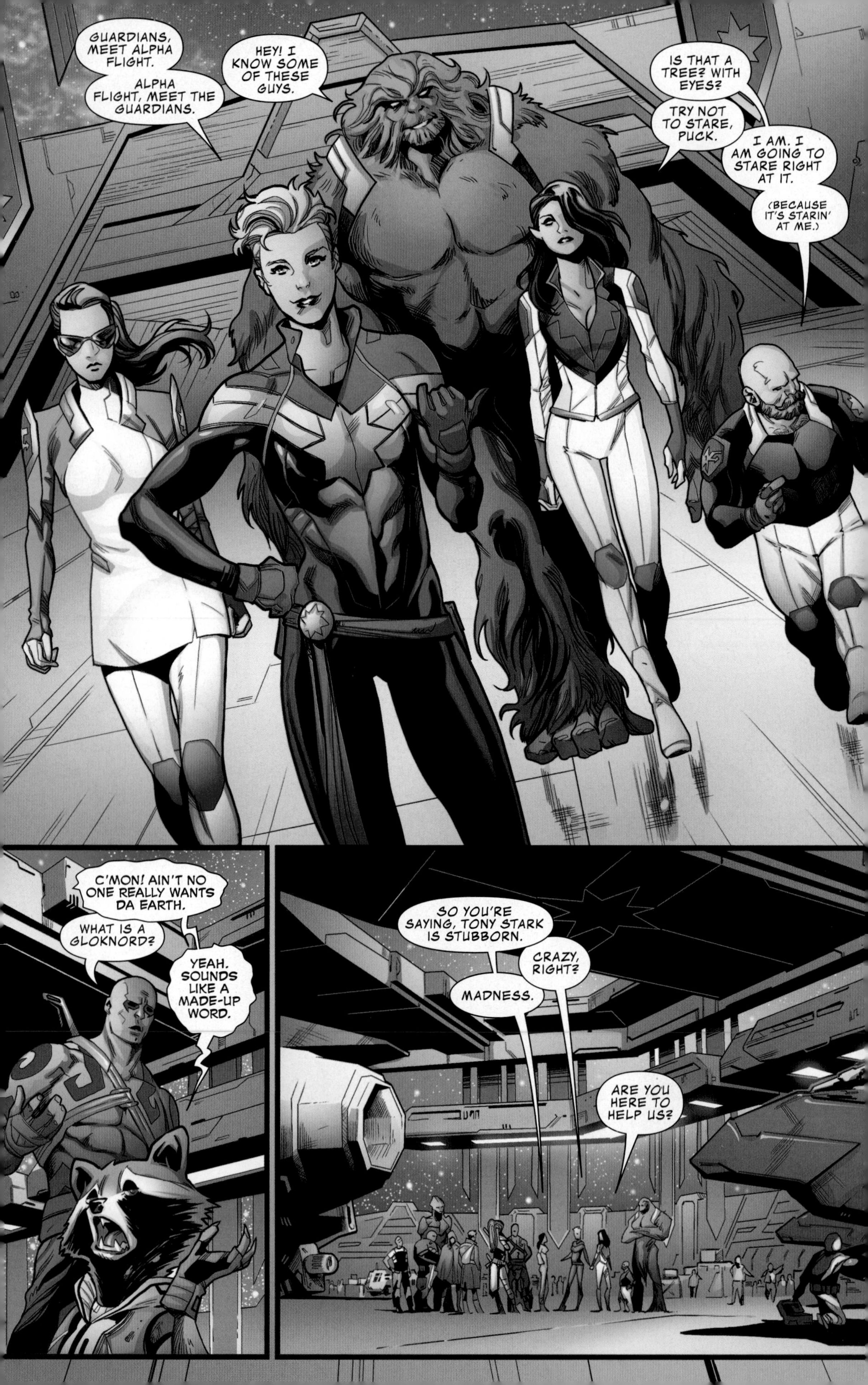
GUARDIANS, MEET ALPHA FLIGHT.
ALPHA FLIGHT, MEET THE GUARDIANS.
HEY! I KNOW SOME OF THESE GUYS.
IS THAT A TREE? WITH EYES?
TRY NOT TO STARE, PUCK.
I AM. I AM GOING TO STARE RIGHT AT IT.
(BECAUSE IT'S STARIN' AT ME.)
C'MON! AIN'T NO ONE REALLY WANTS DA EARTH.
WHAT IS A GLOKNORD?
YEAH. SOUNDS LIKE A MADE-UP WORD.
SO YOU'RE SAYING, TONY STARK IS STUBBORN.
CRAZY, RIGHT?
MADNESS.
ARE YOU HERE TO HELP US?

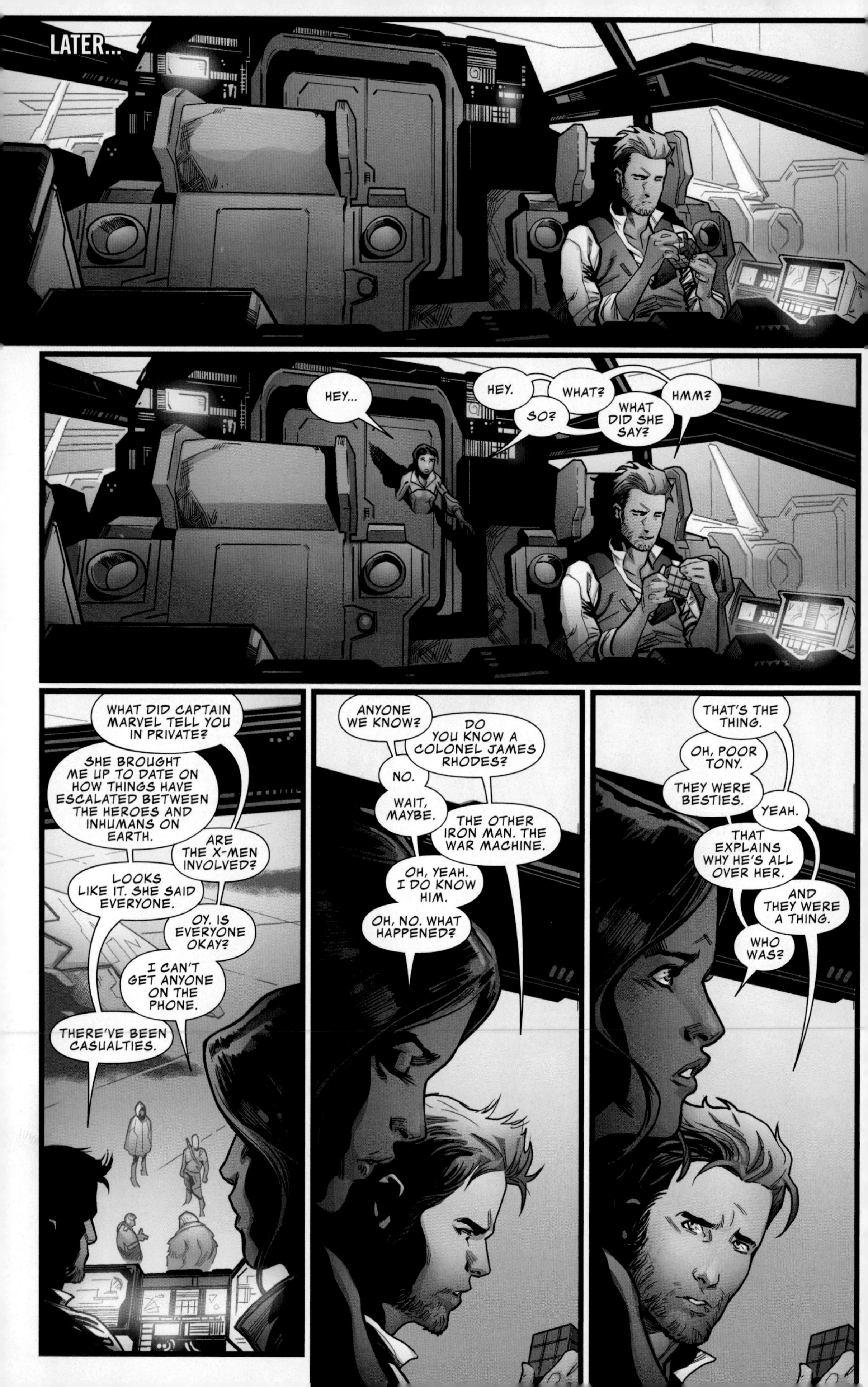
LATER...
HEY...
HEY.
SO?
WHAT?
WHAT DID SHE SAY?
HMM?
WHAT DID CAPTAIN MARVEL TELL YOU IN PRIVATE?
SHE BROUGHT ME UP TO DATE ON HOW THINGS HAVE ESCALATED BETWEEN THE HEROES AND INHUMANS ON EARTH.
ARE THE X-MEN INVOLVED?
LOOKS LIKE IT. SHE SAID EVERYONE.
OY. IS EVERYONE OKAY?
I CAN'T GET ANYONE ON THE PHONE.
THERE'VE BEEN CASUALTIES.
ANYONE WE KNOW?
DO YOU KNOW A COLONEL JAMES RHODES?
NO.
WAIT, MAYBE.
THE OTHER IRON MAN. THE WAR MACHINE.
OH, YEAH. I DO KNOW HIM.
OH, NO. WHAT HAPPENED?
THAT'S THE THING.
OH, POOR TONY.
THEY WERE BESTIES.
YEAH.
THAT EXPLAINS WHY HE'S ALL OVER HER.
AND THEY WERE A THING.
WHO WAS?

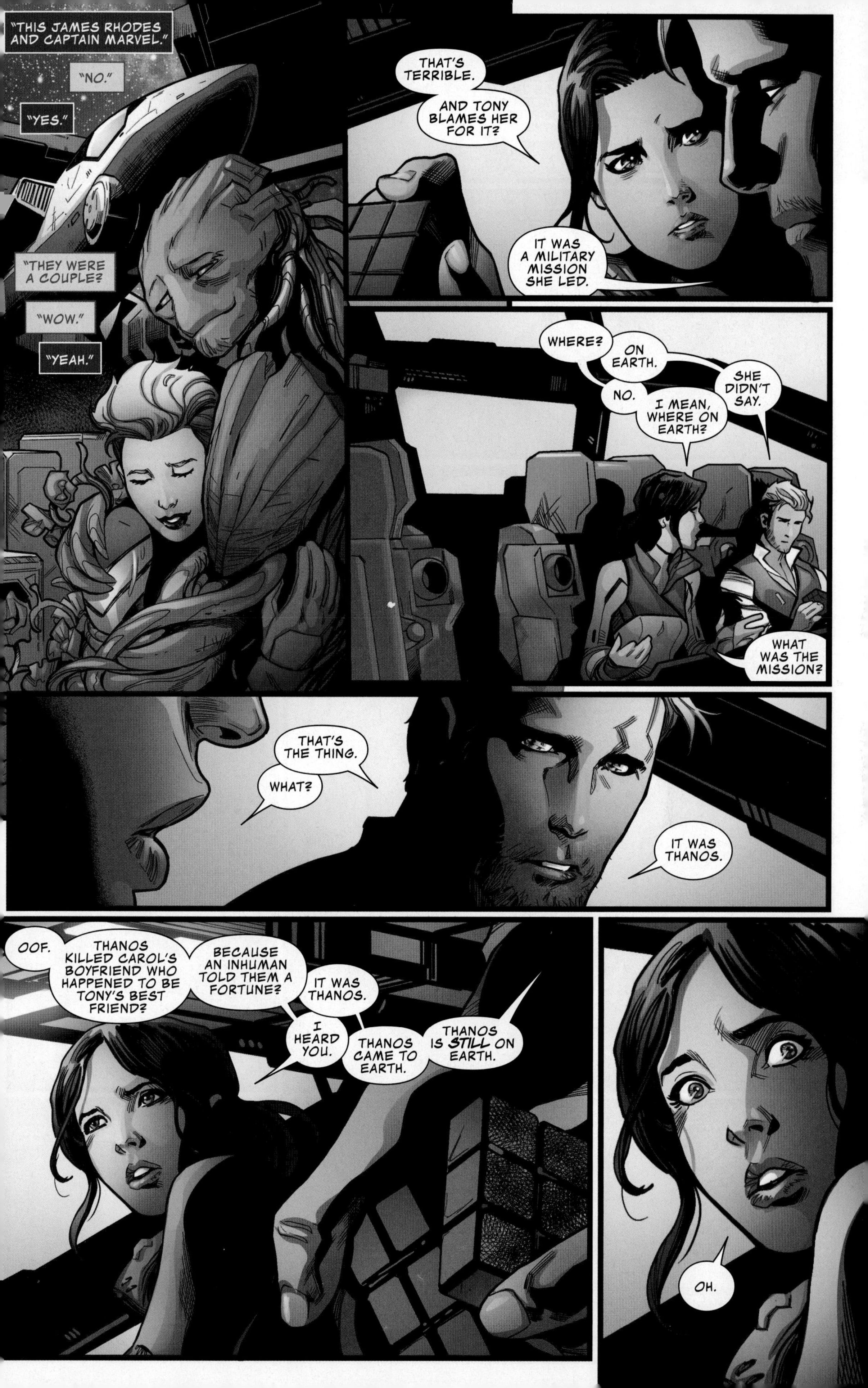
"THIS JAMES RHODES AND CAPTAIN MARVEL."
"NO."
"YES."
"THEY WERE A COUPLE?
"WOW."
"YEAH."
THAT'S TERRIBLE.
AND TONY BLAMES HER FOR IT?
IT WAS A MILITARY MISSION SHE LED.
WHERE?
ON EARTH.
NO.
I MEAN, WHERE ON EARTH?
SHE DIDN'T SAY.
WHAT WAS THE MISSION?
THAT'S THE THING.
WHAT?
IT WAS THANOS.
OOF.
THANOS KILLED CAROL'S BOYFRIEND WHO HAPPENED TO BE TONY'S BEST FRIEND?
BECAUSE AN INHUMAN TOLD THEM A FORTUNE?
IT WAS THANOS.
I HEARD YOU.
THANOS CAME TO EARTH.
THANOS IS STILL ON EARTH.
OH.

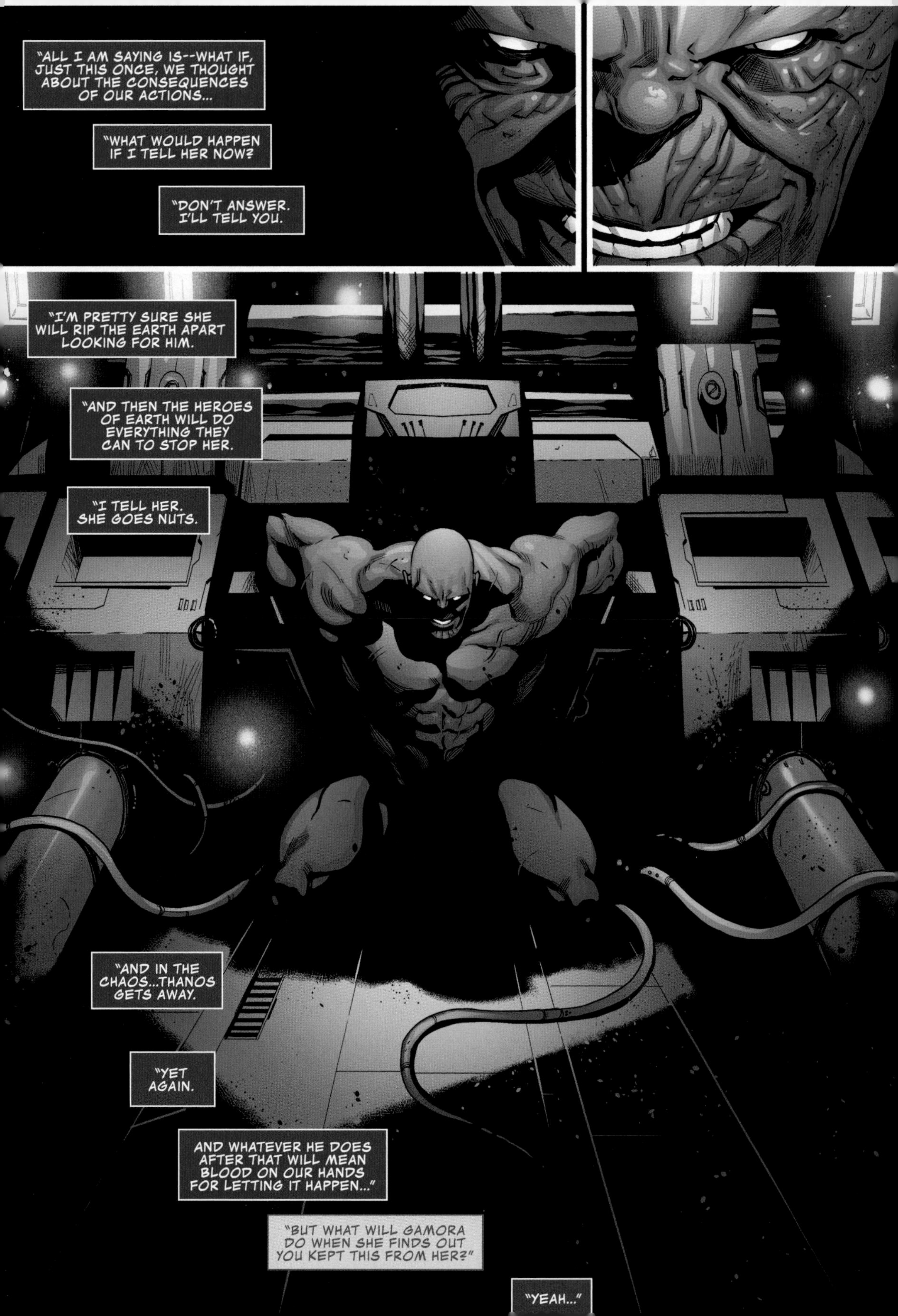
"ALL I AM SAYING IS--WHAT IF, JUST THIS ONCE, WE THOUGHT ABOUT THE CONSEQUENCES OF OUR ACTIONS...
"WHAT WOULD HAPPEN IF I TELL HER NOW?
"DON'T ANSWER. I'LL TELL YOU.
"I'M PRETTY SURE SHE WILL RIP THE EARTH APART LOOKING FOR HIM.
"AND THEN THE HEROES OF EARTH WILL DO EVERYTHING THEY CAN TO STOP HER.
"I TELL HER. SHE GOES NUTS.
"AND IN THE CHAOS...THANOS GETS AWAY.
"YET AGAIN.
AND WHATEVER HE DOES AFTER THAT WILL MEAN BLOOD ON OUR HANDS FOR LETTING IT HAPPEN..."
"BUT WHAT WILL GAMORA DO WHEN SHE FINDS OUT YOU KEPT THIS FROM HER?"
"YEAH..."

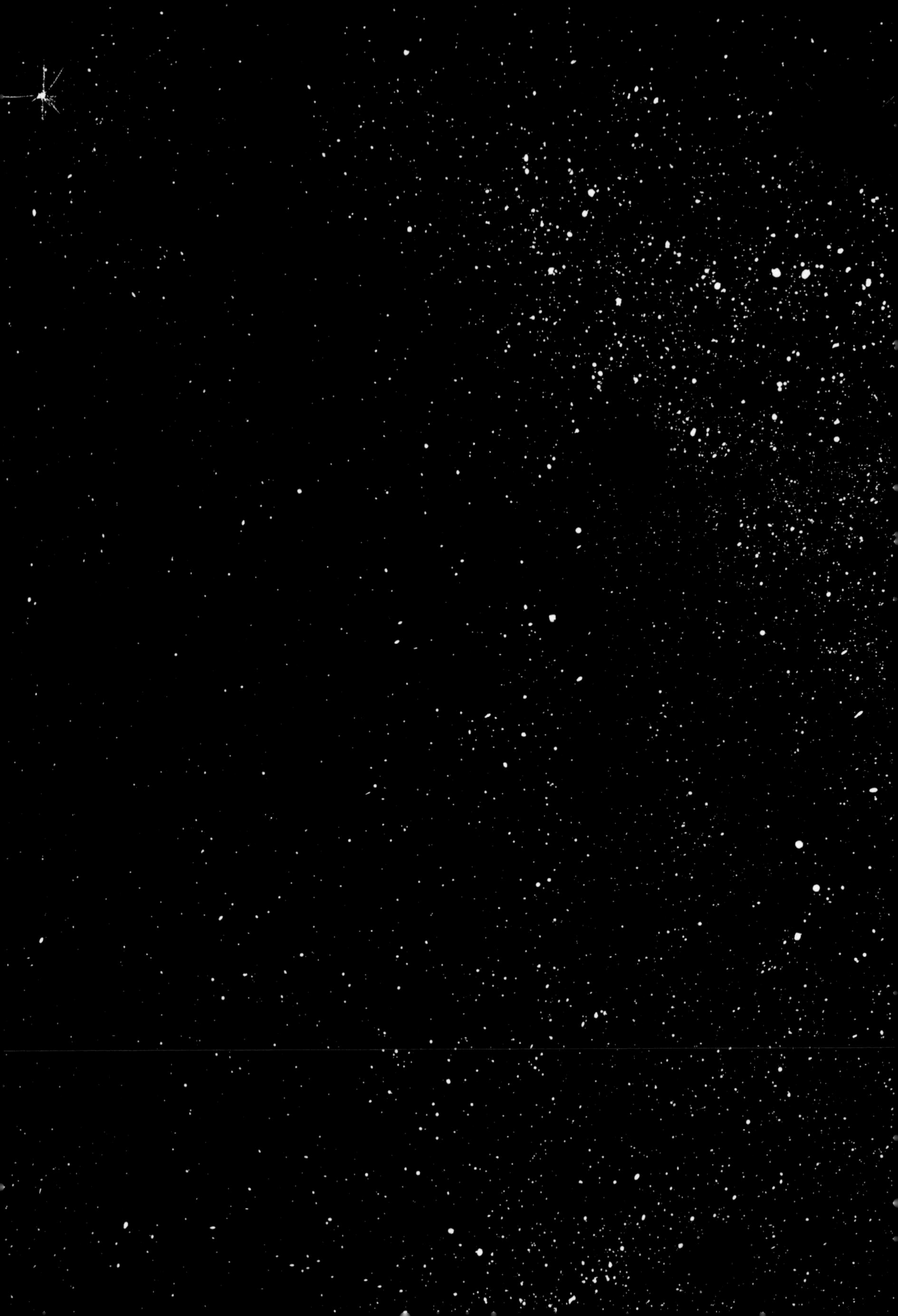

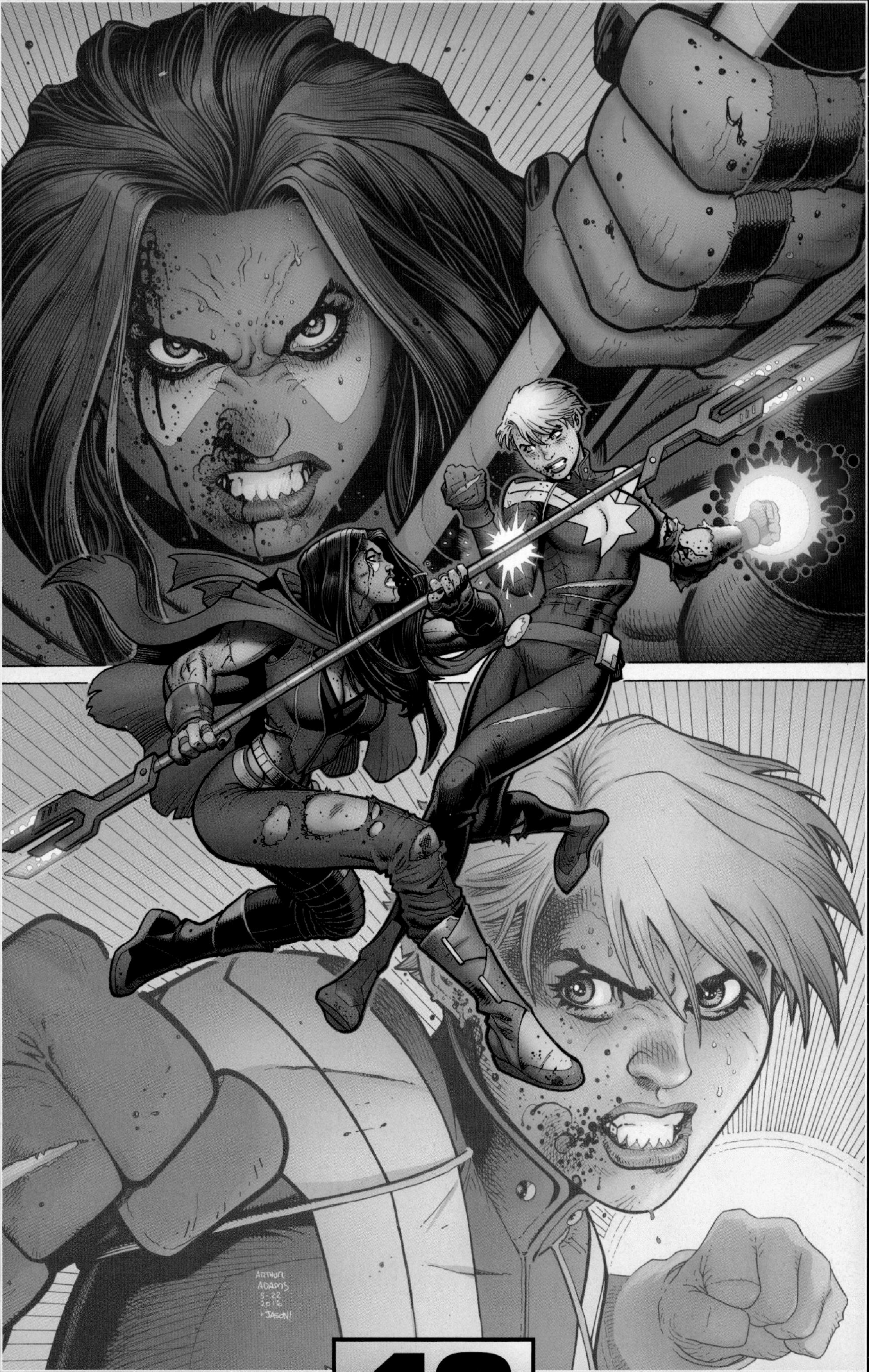
ARTHUR ADAMS 5-22 2016 +JASON!

12

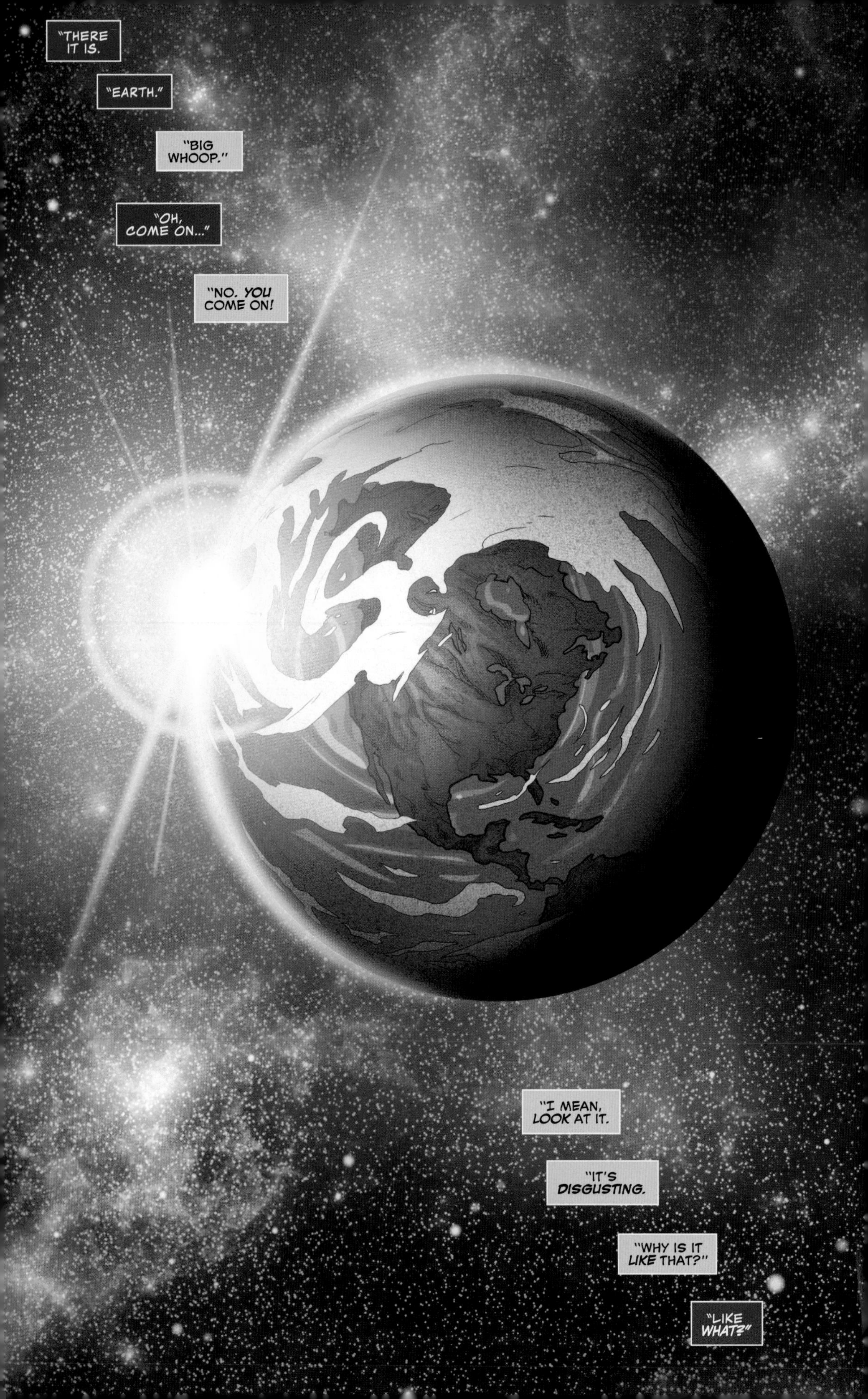
"THERE IT IS.
"EARTH."
"BIG WHOOP."
"OH, COME ON..."
"NO. YOU COME ON!
"I MEAN, LOOK AT IT.
"IT'S DISGUSTING.
"WHY IS IT LIKE THAT?"
"LIKE WHAT?"

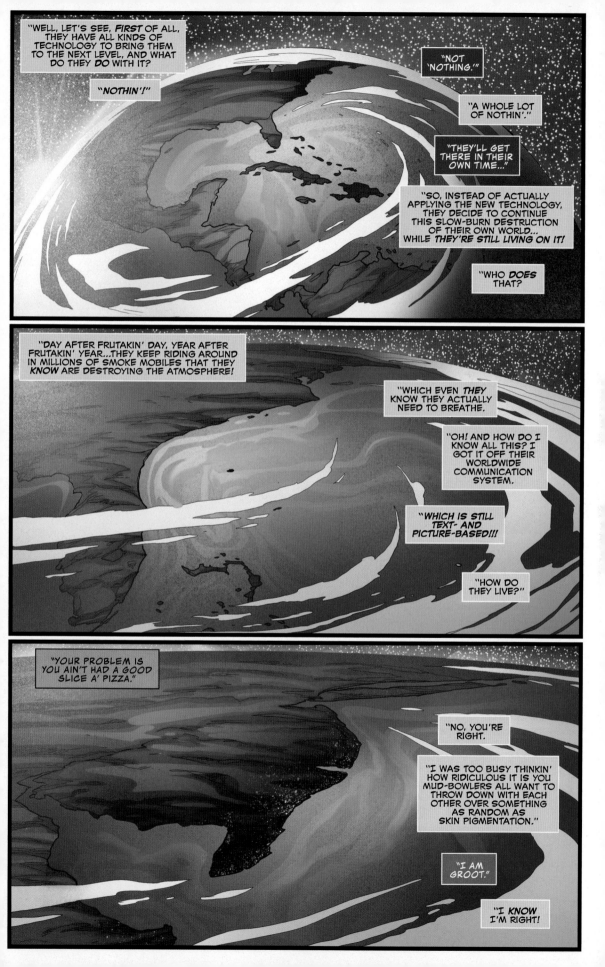

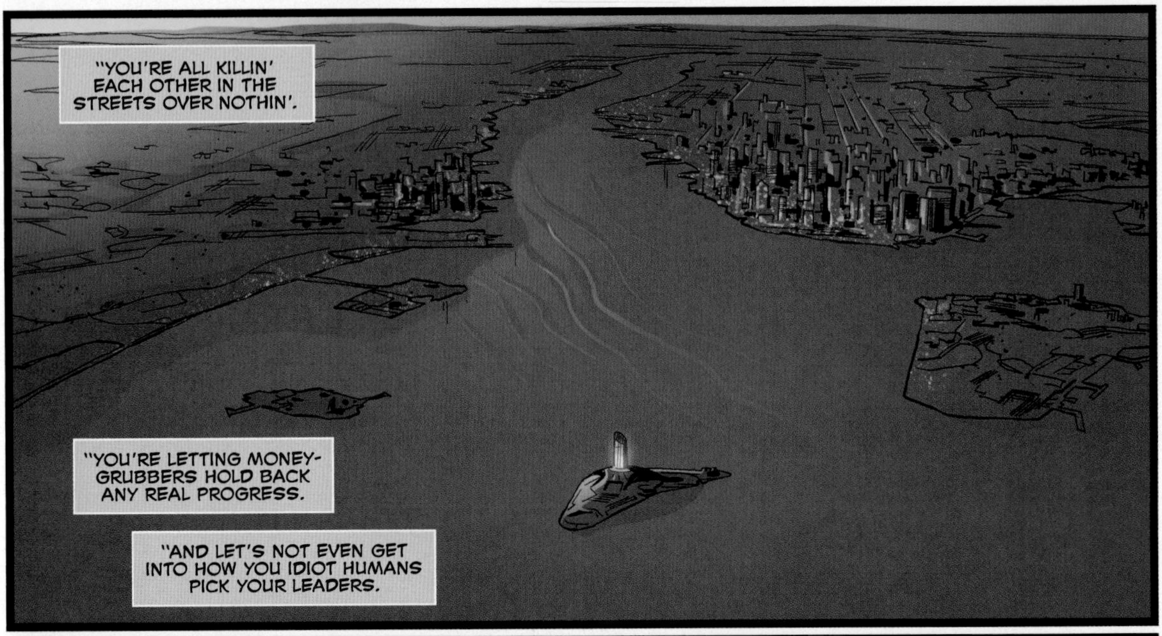
"YOU'RE ALL KILLIN' EACH OTHER IN THE STREETS OVER NOTHIN'.
"YOU'RE LETTING MONEY-GRUBBERS HOLD BACK ANY REAL PROGRESS.
"AND LET'S NOT EVEN GET INTO HOW YOU IDIOT HUMANS PICK YOUR LEADERS.
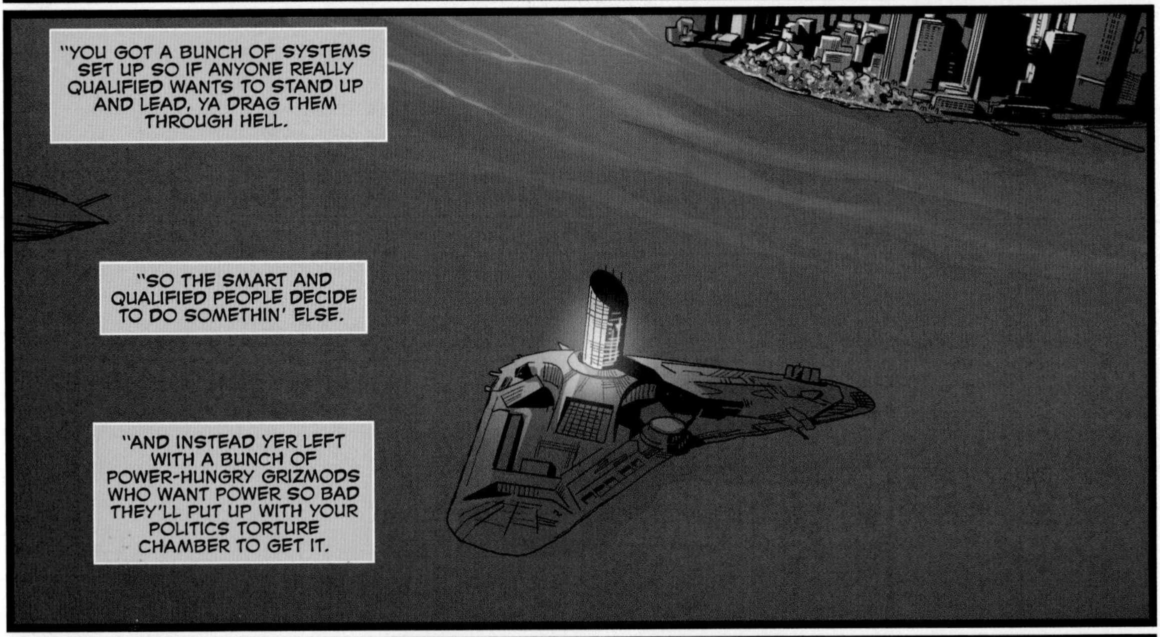
"YOU GOT A BUNCH OF SYSTEMS SET UP SO IF ANYONE REALLY QUALIFIED WANTS TO STAND UP AND LEAD, YA DRAG THEM THROUGH HELL.
"SO THE SMART AND QUALIFIED PEOPLE DECIDE TO DO SOMETHIN' ELSE.
"AND INSTEAD YER LEFT WITH A BUNCH OF POWER-HUNGRY GRIZMODS WHO WANT POWER SO BAD THEY'LL PUT UP WITH YOUR POLITICS TORTURE CHAMBER TO GET IT.
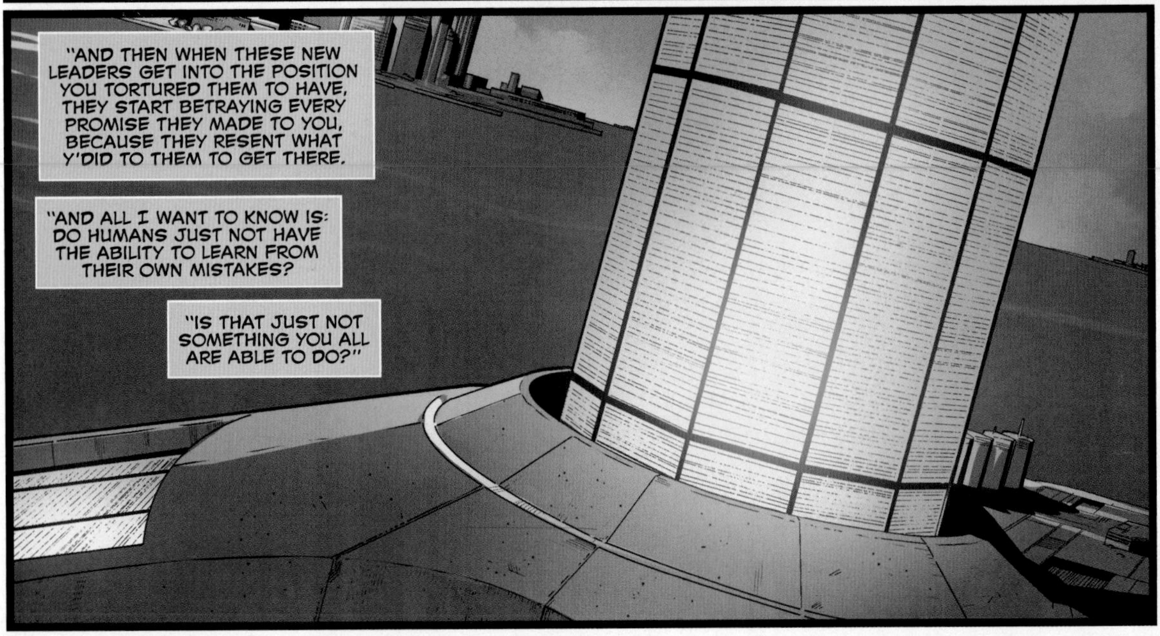
"AND THEN WHEN THESE NEW LEADERS GET INTO THE POSITION YOU TORTURED THEM TO HAVE, THEY START BETRAYING EVERY PROMISE THEY MADE TO YOU, BECAUSE THEY RESENT WHAT Y'DID TO THEM TO GET THERE.
"AND ALL I WANT TO KNOW IS: DO HUMANS JUST NOT HAVE THE ABILITY TO LEARN FROM THEIR OWN MISTAKES?
"IS THAT JUST NOT SOMETHING YOU ALL ARE ABLE TO DO?"

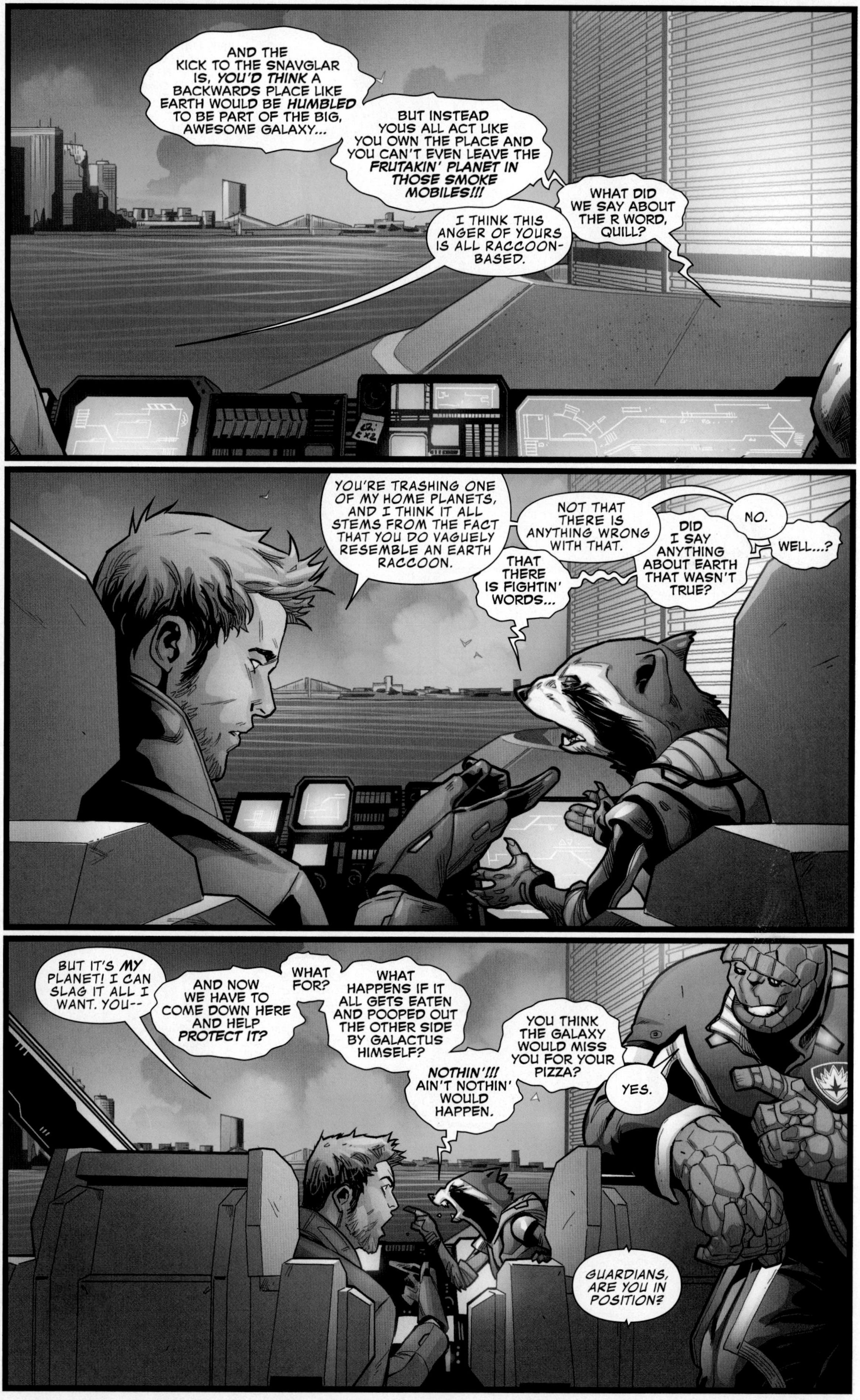
AND THE KICK TO THE SNAVGLAR IS, *YOU'D THINK* A BACKWARDS PLACE LIKE EARTH WOULD BE *HUMBLED* TO BE PART OF THE BIG, AWESOME GALAXY...
BUT INSTEAD YOUS ALL ACT LIKE YOU OWN THE PLACE AND YOU CAN'T EVEN LEAVE THE *FRUTAKIN' PLANET IN THOSE SMOKE MOBILES!!!*
I THINK THIS ANGER OF YOURS IS ALL RACCOON-BASED.
WHAT DID WE SAY ABOUT THE R WORD, QUILL?
YOU'RE TRASHING ONE OF MY HOME PLANETS, AND I THINK IT ALL STEMS FROM THE FACT THAT YOU DO VAGUELY RESEMBLE AN EARTH RACCOON.
NOT THAT THERE IS ANYTHING WRONG WITH THAT.
NO.
THAT THERE IS FIGHTIN' WORDS...
DID I SAY ANYTHING ABOUT EARTH THAT WASN'T TRUE?
WELL...?
BUT IT'S *MY* PLANET! I CAN SLAG IT ALL I WANT. YOU--
AND NOW WE HAVE TO COME DOWN HERE AND HELP *PROTECT IT?*
WHAT FOR?
WHAT HAPPENS IF IT ALL GETS EATEN AND POOPED OUT THE OTHER SIDE BY GALACTUS HIMSELF?
NOTHIN'!!! AIN'T NOTHIN' WOULD HAPPEN.
YOU THINK THE GALAXY WOULD MISS YOU FOR YOUR PIZZA?
YES.
GUARDIANS, ARE YOU IN POSITION?

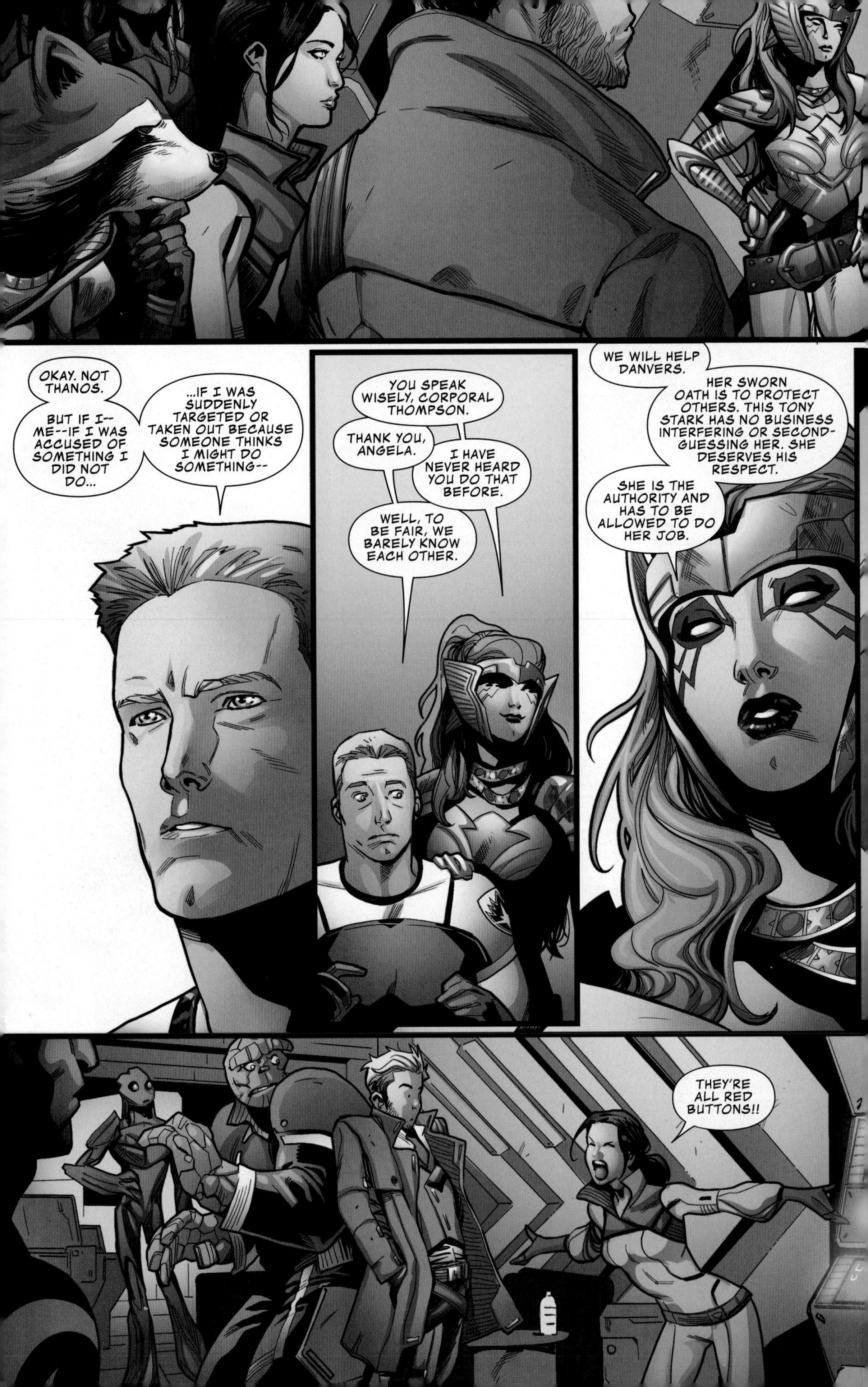
OKAY. NOT THANOS.
BUT IF I-- ME--IF I WAS ACCUSED OF SOMETHING I DID NOT DO...
...IF I WAS SUDDENLY TARGETED OR TAKEN OUT BECAUSE SOMEONE THINKS I MIGHT DO SOMETHING--
YOU SPEAK WISELY, CORPORAL THOMPSON.
THANK YOU, ANGELA.
I HAVE NEVER HEARD YOU DO THAT BEFORE.
WELL, TO BE FAIR, WE BARELY KNOW EACH OTHER.
WE WILL HELP DANVERS.
HER SWORN OATH IS TO PROTECT OTHERS. THIS TONY STARK HAS NO BUSINESS INTERFERING OR SECOND-GUESSING HER. SHE DESERVES HIS RESPECT.
SHE IS THE AUTHORITY AND HAS TO BE ALLOWED TO DO HER JOB.
THEY'RE ALL RED BUTTONS!!

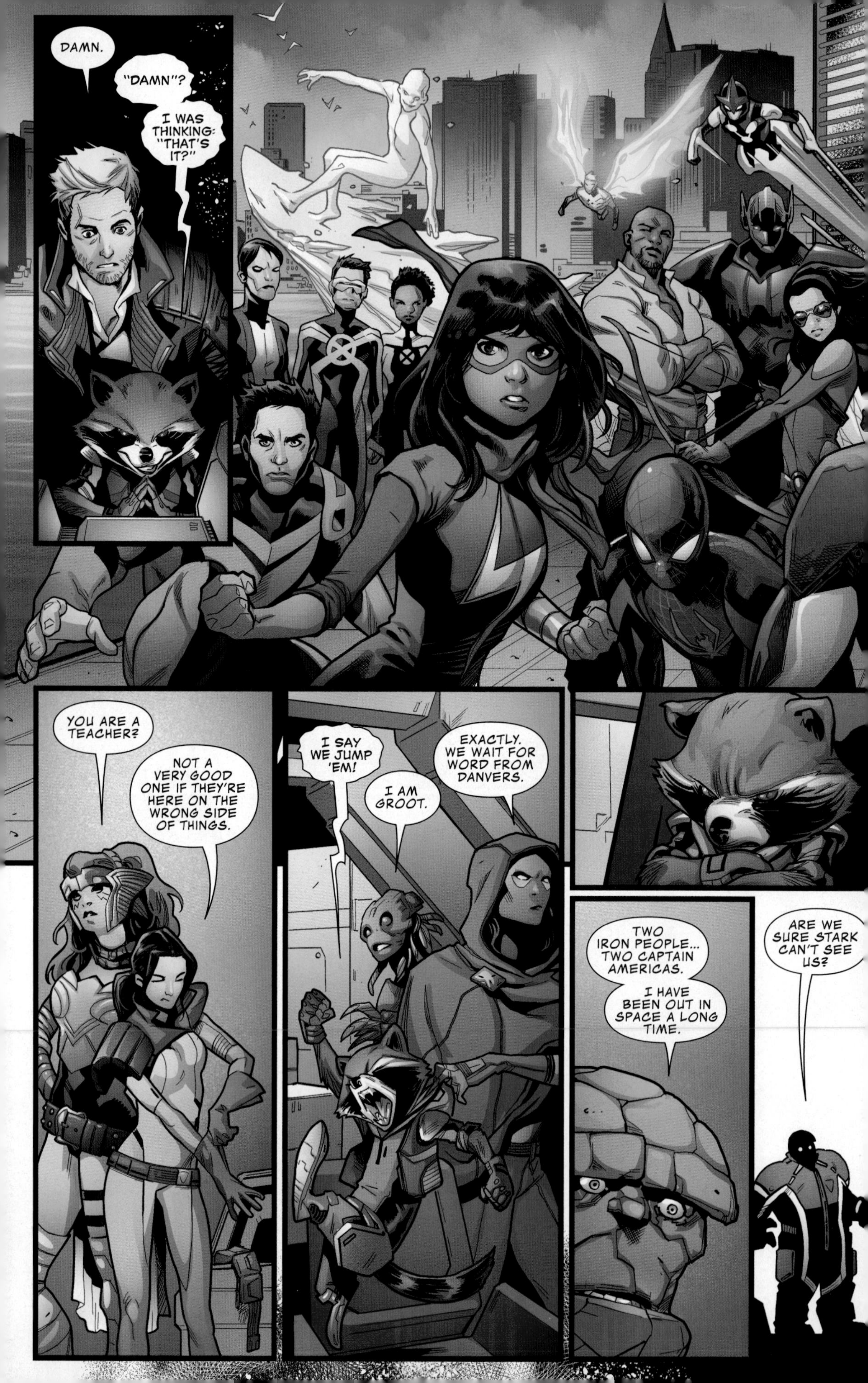
DAMN.
"DAMN"?
I WAS THINKING: "THAT'S IT?"
YOU ARE A TEACHER?
NOT A VERY GOOD ONE IF THEY'RE HERE ON THE WRONG SIDE OF THINGS.
I SAY WE JUMP 'EM!
I AM GROOT.
EXACTLY. WE WAIT FOR WORD FROM DANVERS.
TWO IRON PEOPLE... TWO CAPTAIN AMERICAS.
I HAVE BEEN OUT IN SPACE A LONG TIME.
ARE WE SURE STARK CAN'T SEE US?

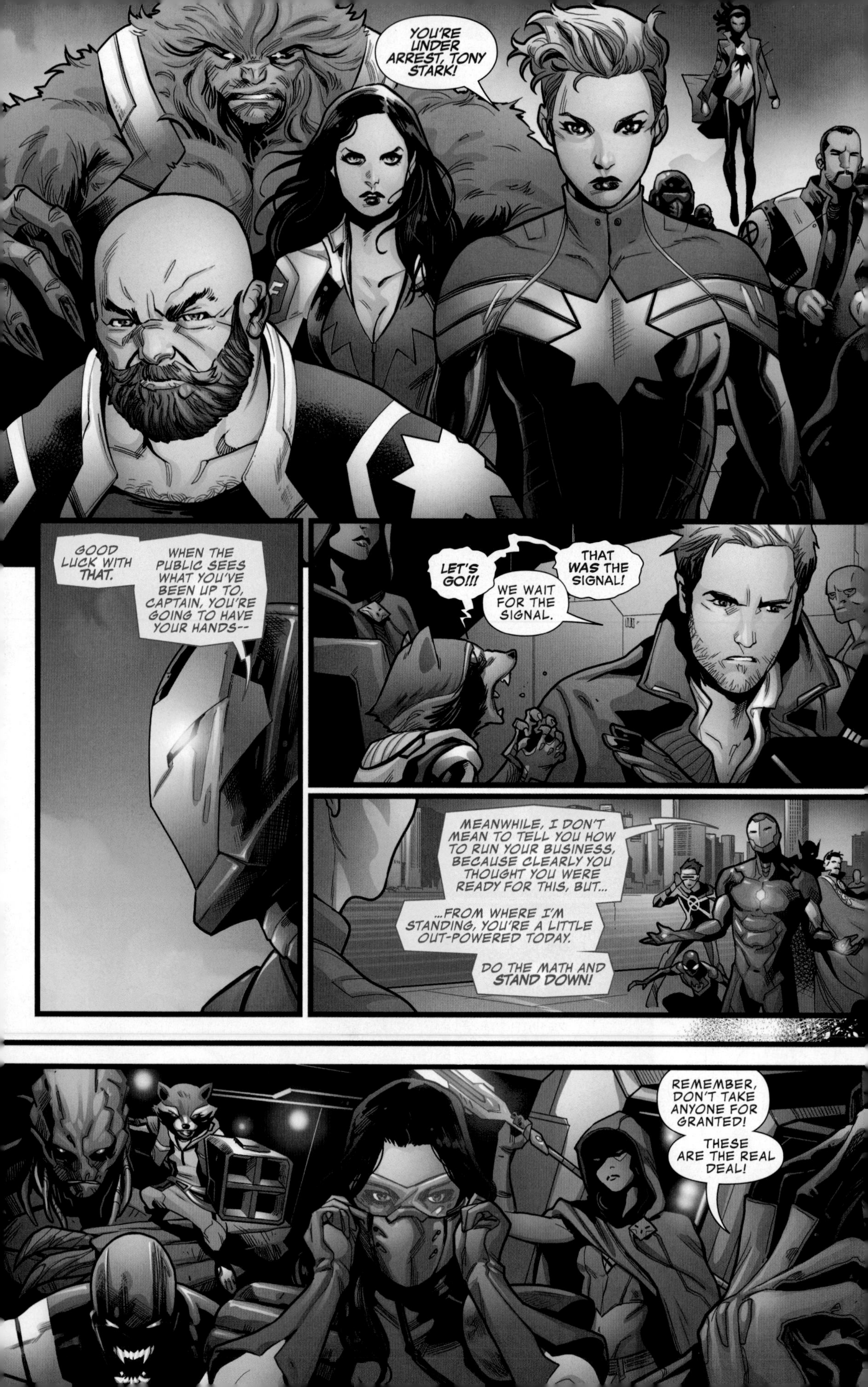
YOU'RE UNDER ARREST, TONY STARK!
GOOD LUCK WITH THAT.
WHEN THE PUBLIC SEES WHAT YOU'VE BEEN UP TO, CAPTAIN, YOU'RE GOING TO HAVE YOUR HANDS--
LET'S GO!!!
WE WAIT FOR THE SIGNAL.
THAT WAS THE SIGNAL!
MEANWHILE, I DON'T MEAN TO TELL YOU HOW TO RUN YOUR BUSINESS, BECAUSE CLEARLY YOU THOUGHT YOU WERE READY FOR THIS, BUT...
...FROM WHERE I'M STANDING, YOU'RE A LITTLE OUT-POWERED TODAY.
DO THE MATH AND STAND DOWN!
REMEMBER, DON'T TAKE ANYONE FOR GRANTED!
THESE ARE THE REAL DEAL!

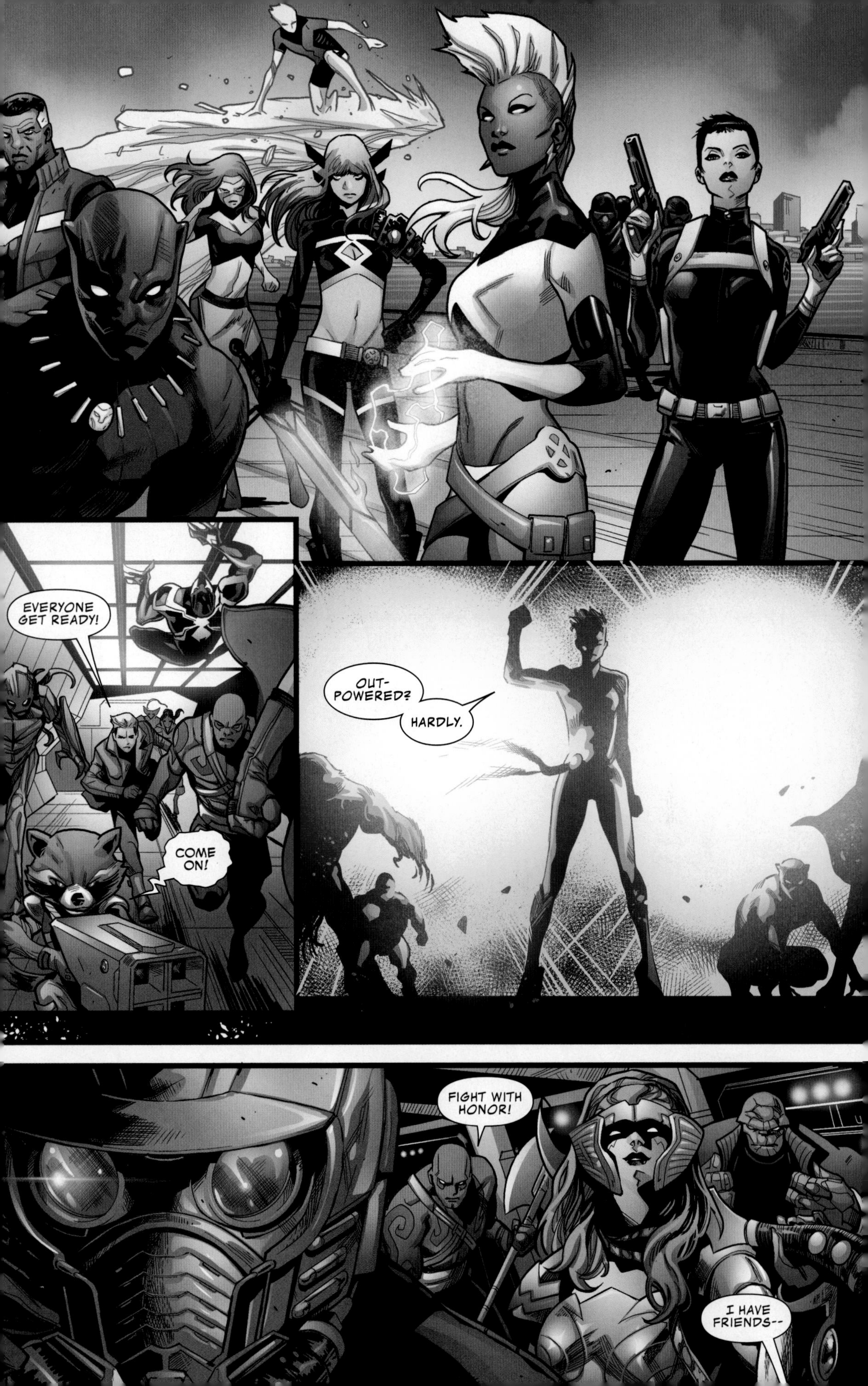
EVERYONE GET READY!
COME ON!
OUT-POWERED?
HARDLY.
FIGHT WITH HONOR!
I HAVE FRIENDS--

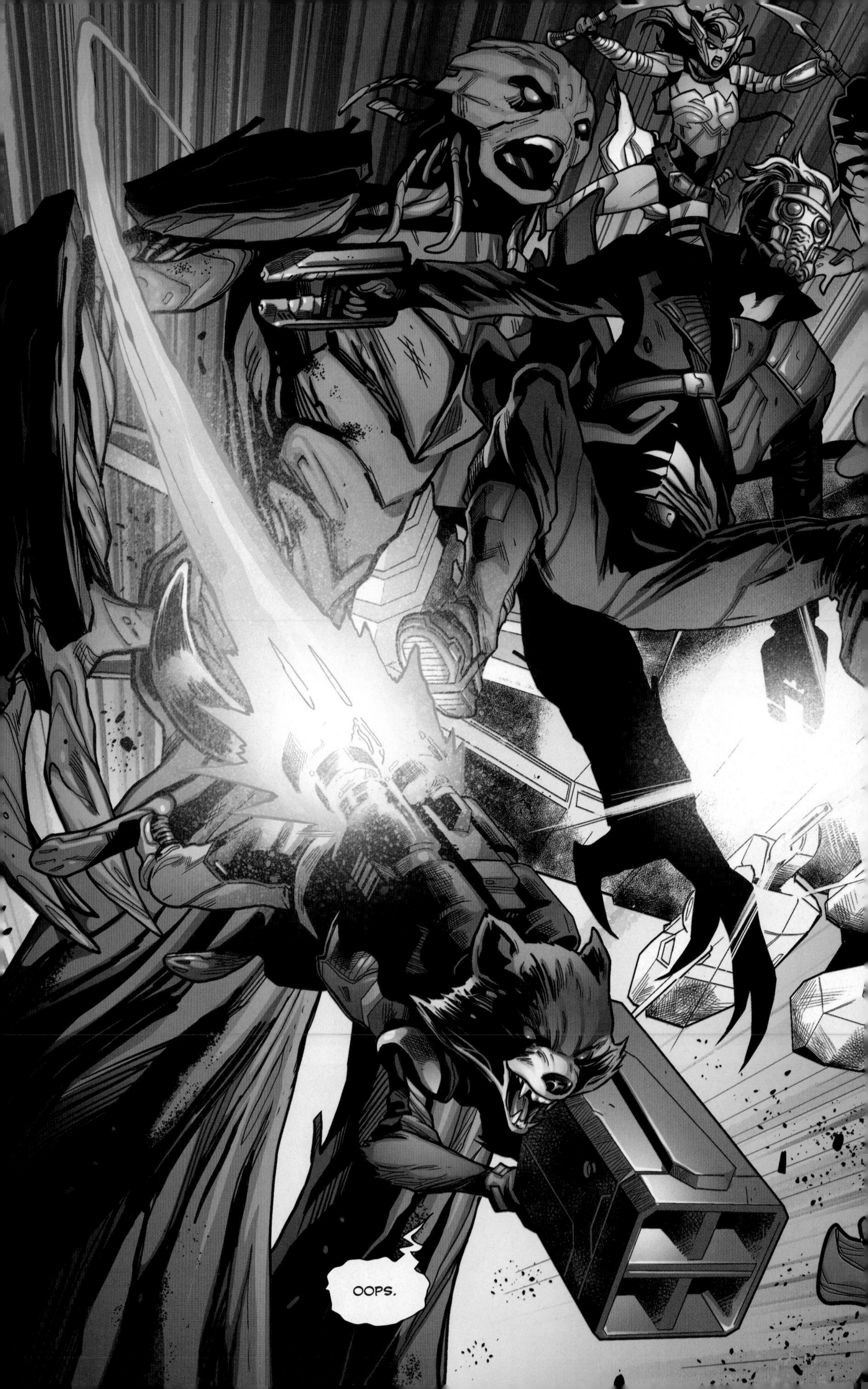
OOPS.

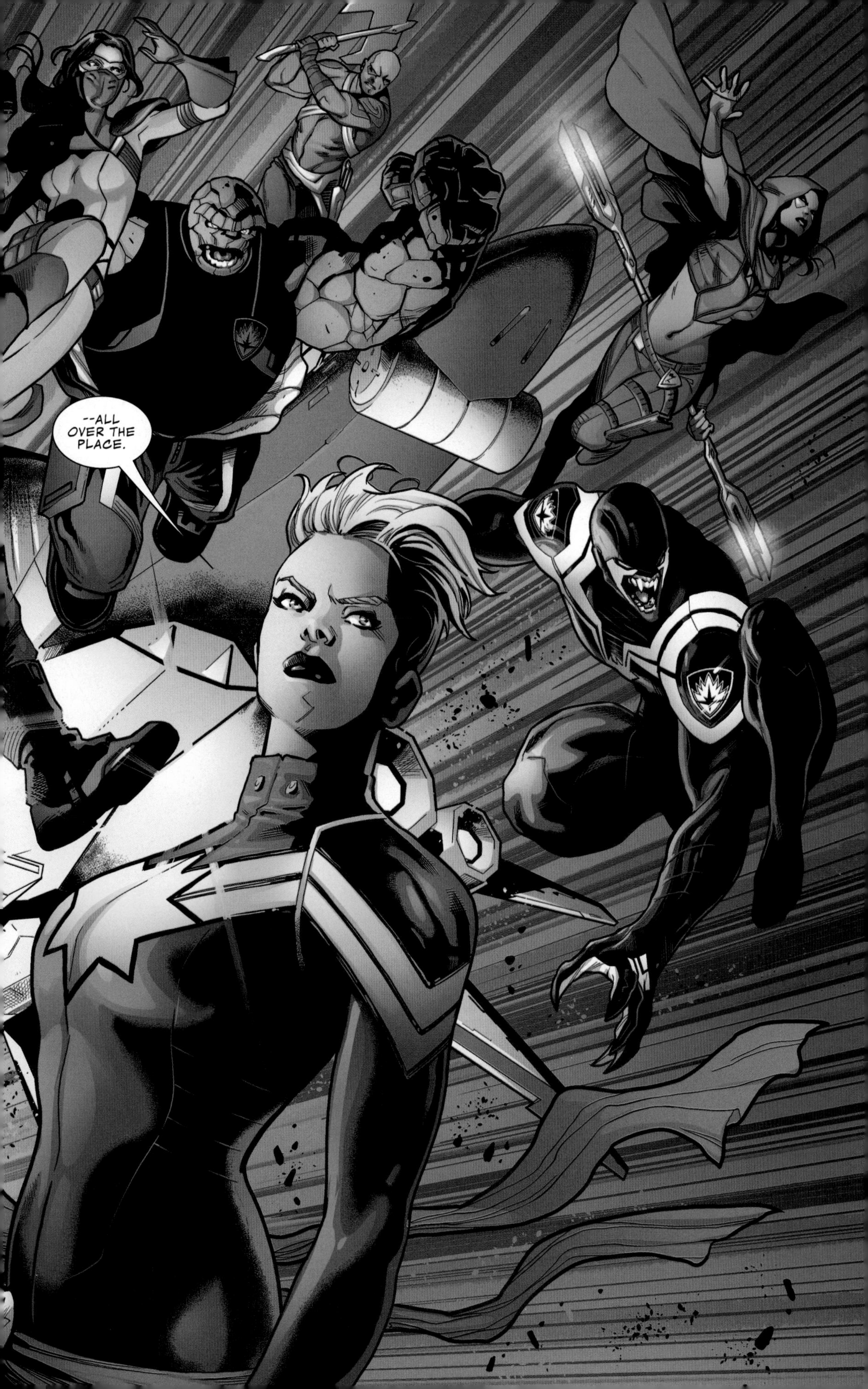
--ALL OVER THE PLACE.

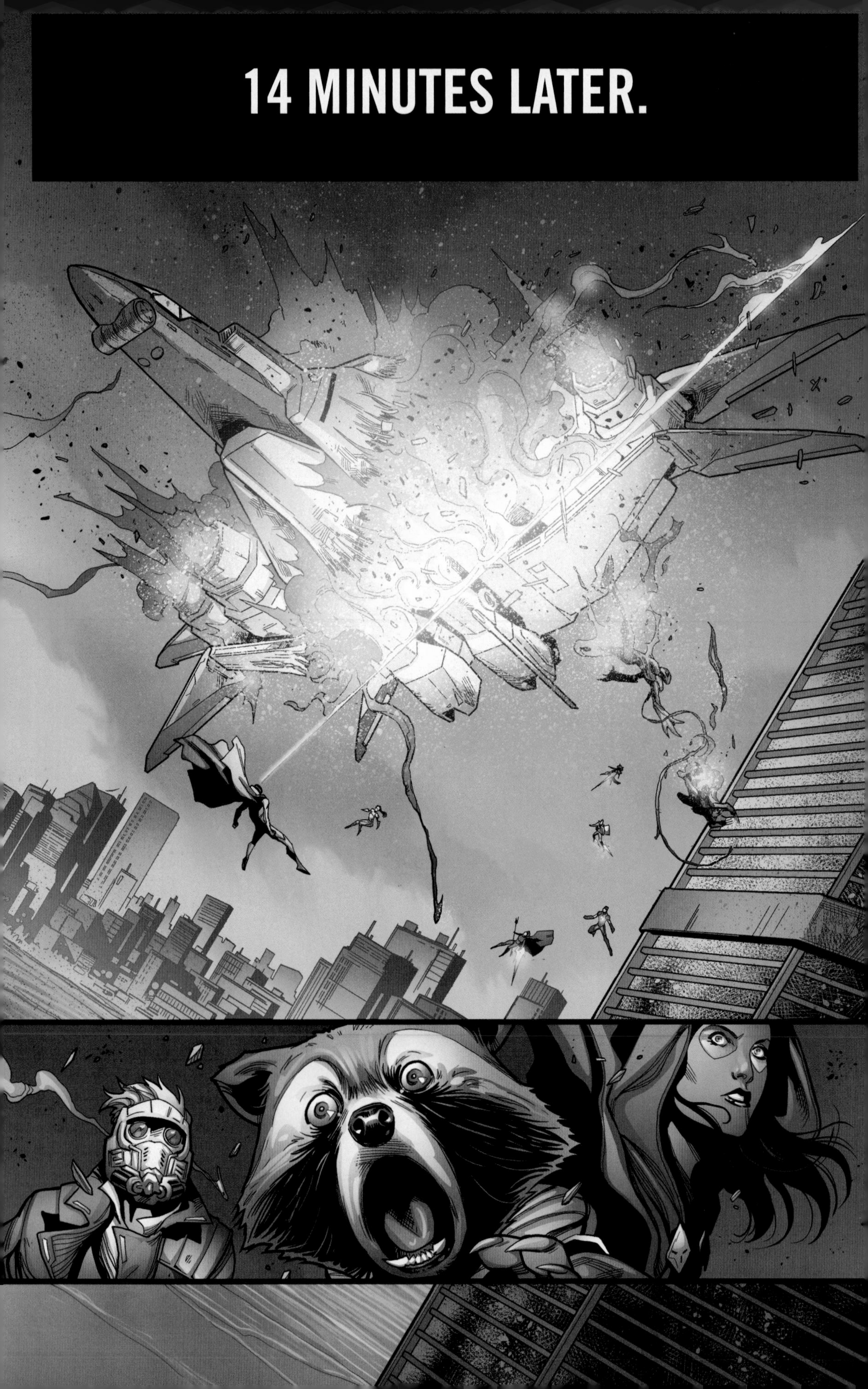
14 MINUTES LATER.

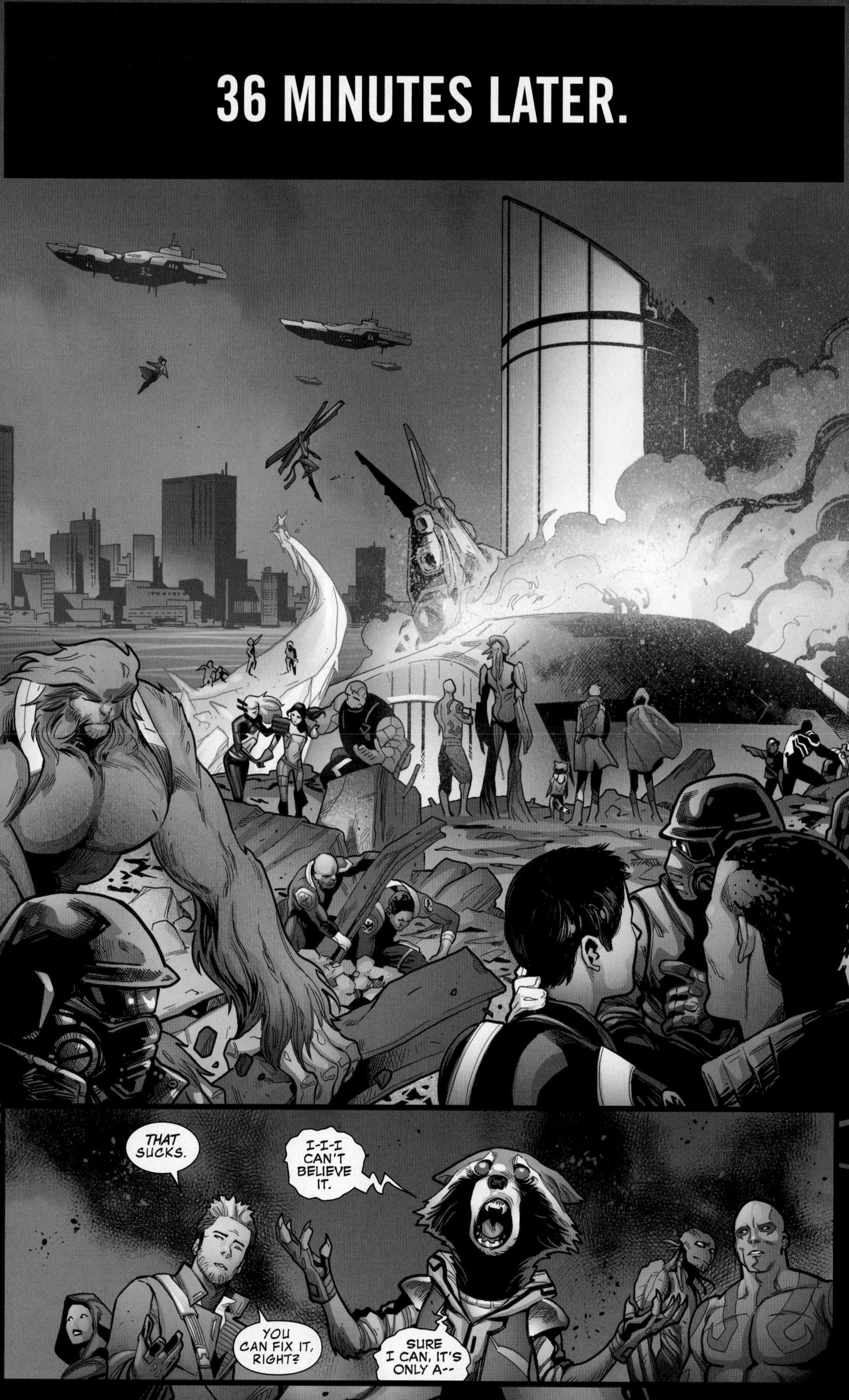
36 MINUTES LATER.
THAT SUCKS.
I-I-I CAN'T BELIEVE IT.
YOU CAN FIX IT, RIGHT?
SURE I CAN, IT'S ONLY A--

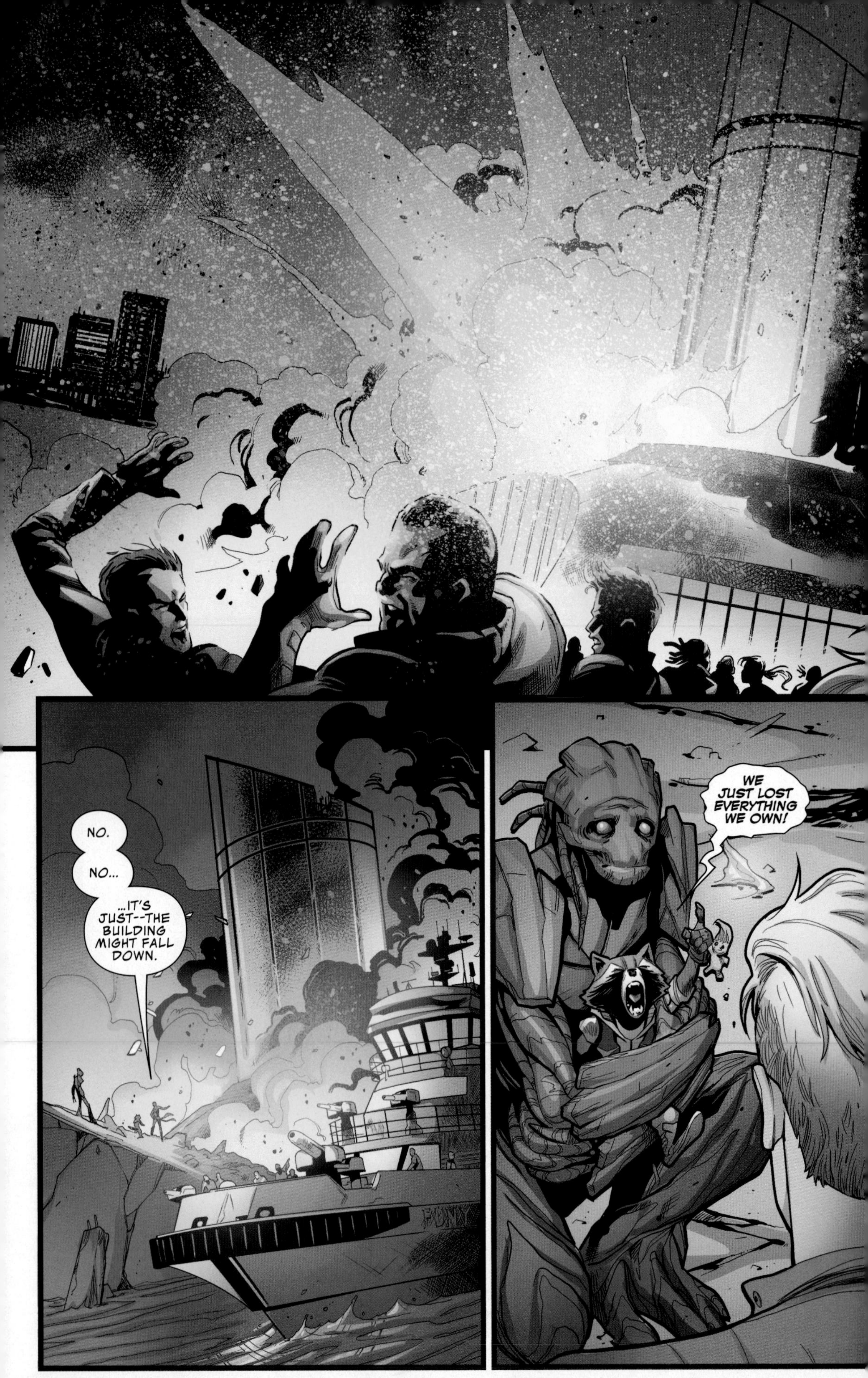
NO.
NO...
...IT'S JUST--THE BUILDING MIGHT FALL DOWN.
WE JUST LOST EVERYTHING WE OWN!

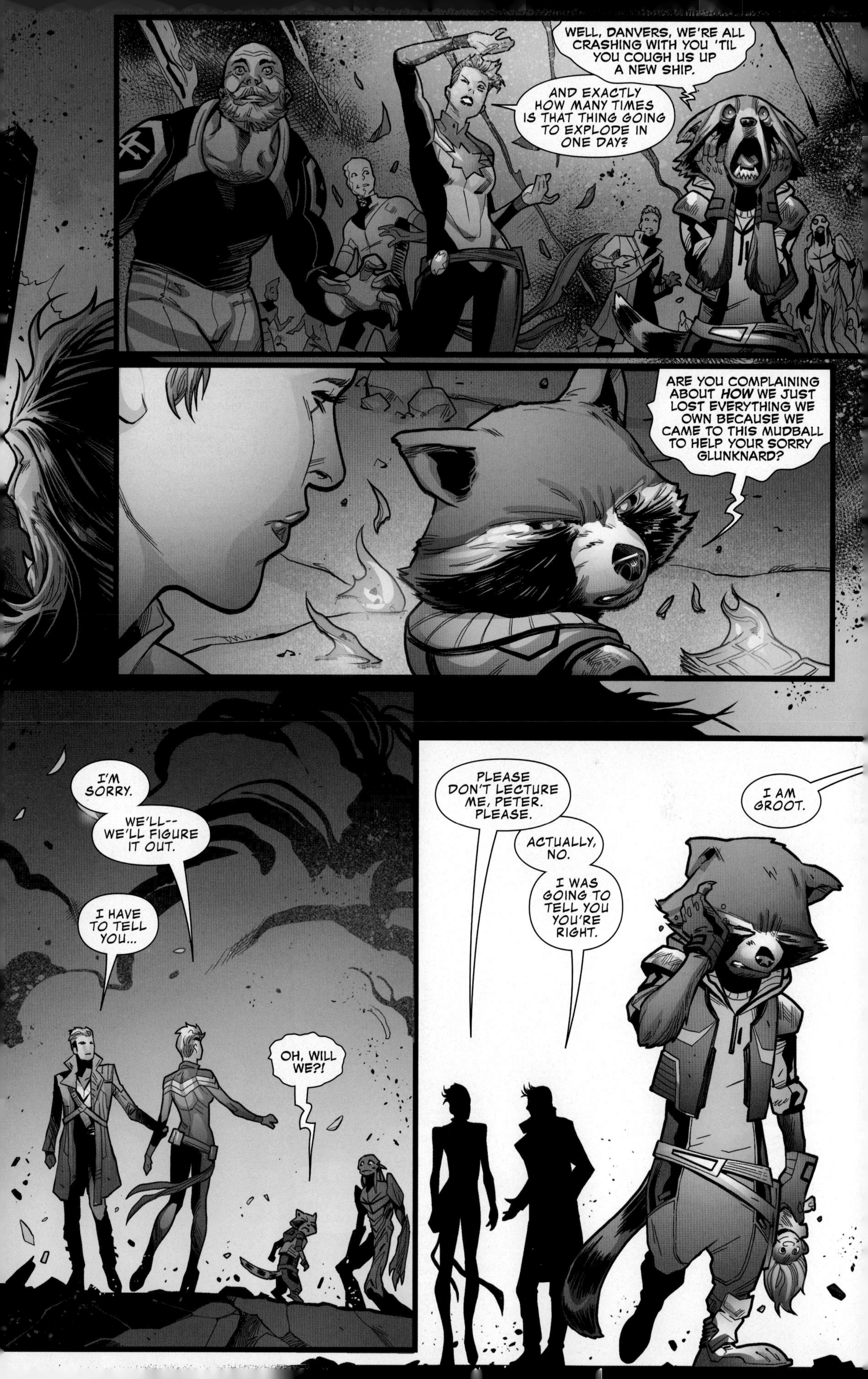
WELL, DANVERS, WE'RE ALL CRASHING WITH YOU 'TIL YOU COUGH US UP A NEW SHIP.
AND EXACTLY HOW MANY TIMES IS THAT THING GOING TO EXPLODE IN ONE DAY?
ARE YOU COMPLAINING ABOUT *HOW* WE JUST LOST EVERYTHING WE OWN BECAUSE WE CAME TO THIS MUDBALL TO HELP YOUR SORRY GLUNKNARD?
I'M SORRY.
WE'LL-- WE'LL FIGURE IT OUT.
I HAVE TO TELL YOU...
OH, WILL WE?!
PLEASE DON'T LECTURE ME, PETER. PLEASE.
ACTUALLY, NO.
I WAS GOING TO TELL YOU YOU'RE RIGHT.
I AM GROOT.

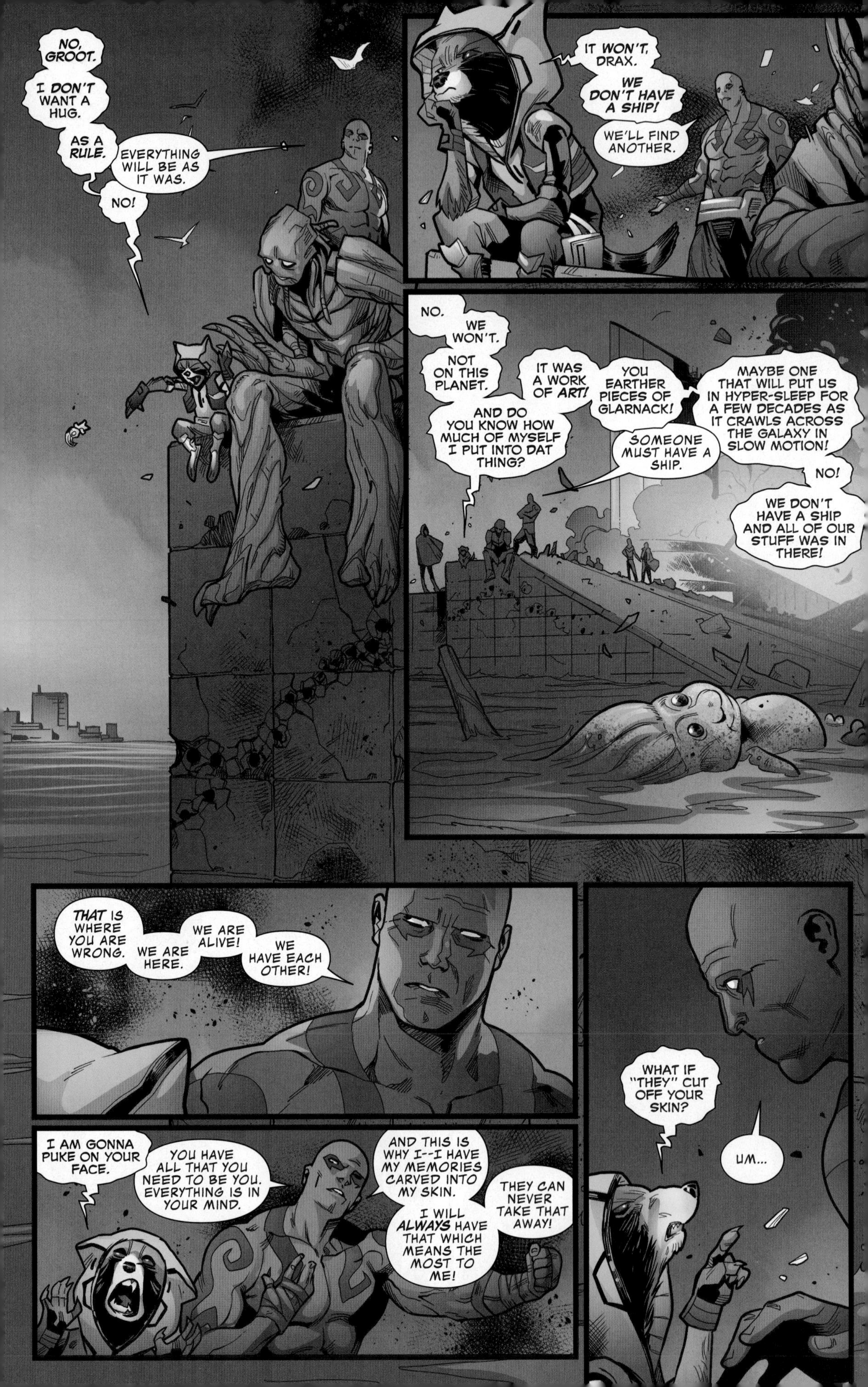
NO, GROOT.
I DON'T WANT A HUG.
AS A RULE.
EVERYTHING WILL BE AS IT WAS.
NO!
IT WON'T, DRAX.
WE DON'T HAVE A SHIP!
WE'LL FIND ANOTHER.
NO.
WE WON'T.
NOT ON THIS PLANET.
IT WAS A WORK OF ART!
AND DO YOU KNOW HOW MUCH OF MYSELF I PUT INTO DAT THING?
YOU EARTHER PIECES OF GLARNACK!
SOMEONE MUST HAVE A SHIP.
MAYBE ONE THAT WILL PUT US IN HYPER-SLEEP FOR A FEW DECADES AS IT CRAWLS ACROSS THE GALAXY IN SLOW MOTION!
NO!
WE DON'T HAVE A SHIP AND ALL OF OUR STUFF WAS IN THERE!
THAT IS WHERE YOU ARE WRONG.
WE ARE HERE.
WE ARE ALIVE!
WE HAVE EACH OTHER!
I AM GONNA PUKE ON YOUR FACE.
YOU HAVE ALL THAT YOU NEED TO BE YOU. EVERYTHING IS IN YOUR MIND.
AND THIS IS WHY I--I HAVE MY MEMORIES CARVED INTO MY SKIN.
I WILL ALWAYS HAVE THAT WHICH MEANS THE MOST TO ME!
THEY CAN NEVER TAKE THAT AWAY!
WHAT IF "THEY" CUT OFF YOUR SKIN?
UM...

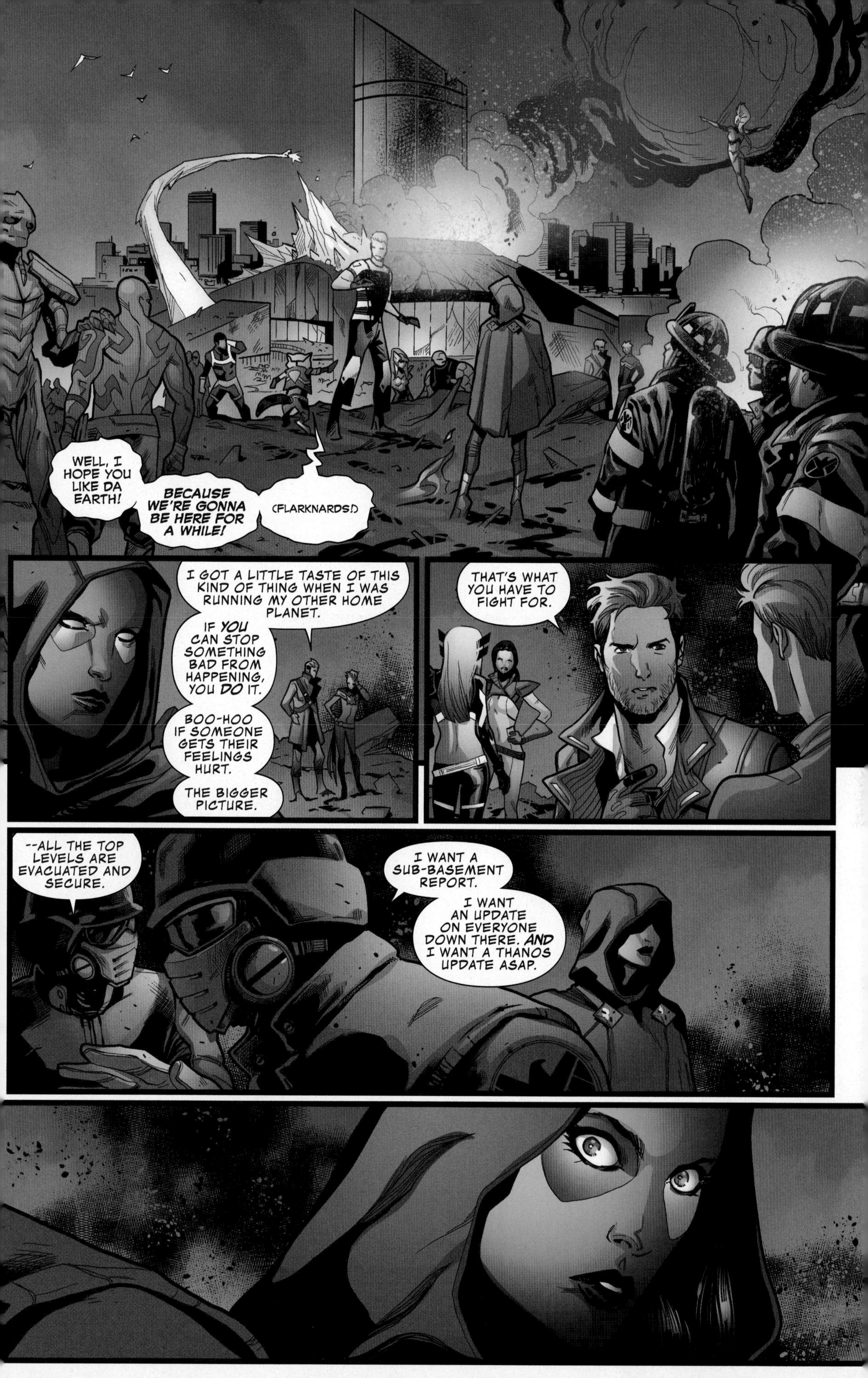
WELL, I HOPE YOU LIKE DA EARTH!
BECAUSE WE'RE GONNA BE HERE FOR A WHILE!
(FLARKNARDS!)
I GOT A LITTLE TASTE OF THIS KIND OF THING WHEN I WAS RUNNING MY OTHER HOME PLANET.
IF YOU CAN STOP SOMETHING BAD FROM HAPPENING, YOU DO IT.
BOO-HOO IF SOMEONE GETS THEIR FEELINGS HURT.
THE BIGGER PICTURE.
THAT'S WHAT YOU HAVE TO FIGHT FOR.
--ALL THE TOP LEVELS ARE EVACUATED AND SECURE.
I WANT A SUB-BASEMENT REPORT.
I WANT AN UPDATE ON EVERYONE DOWN THERE. AND I WANT A THANOS UPDATE ASAP.

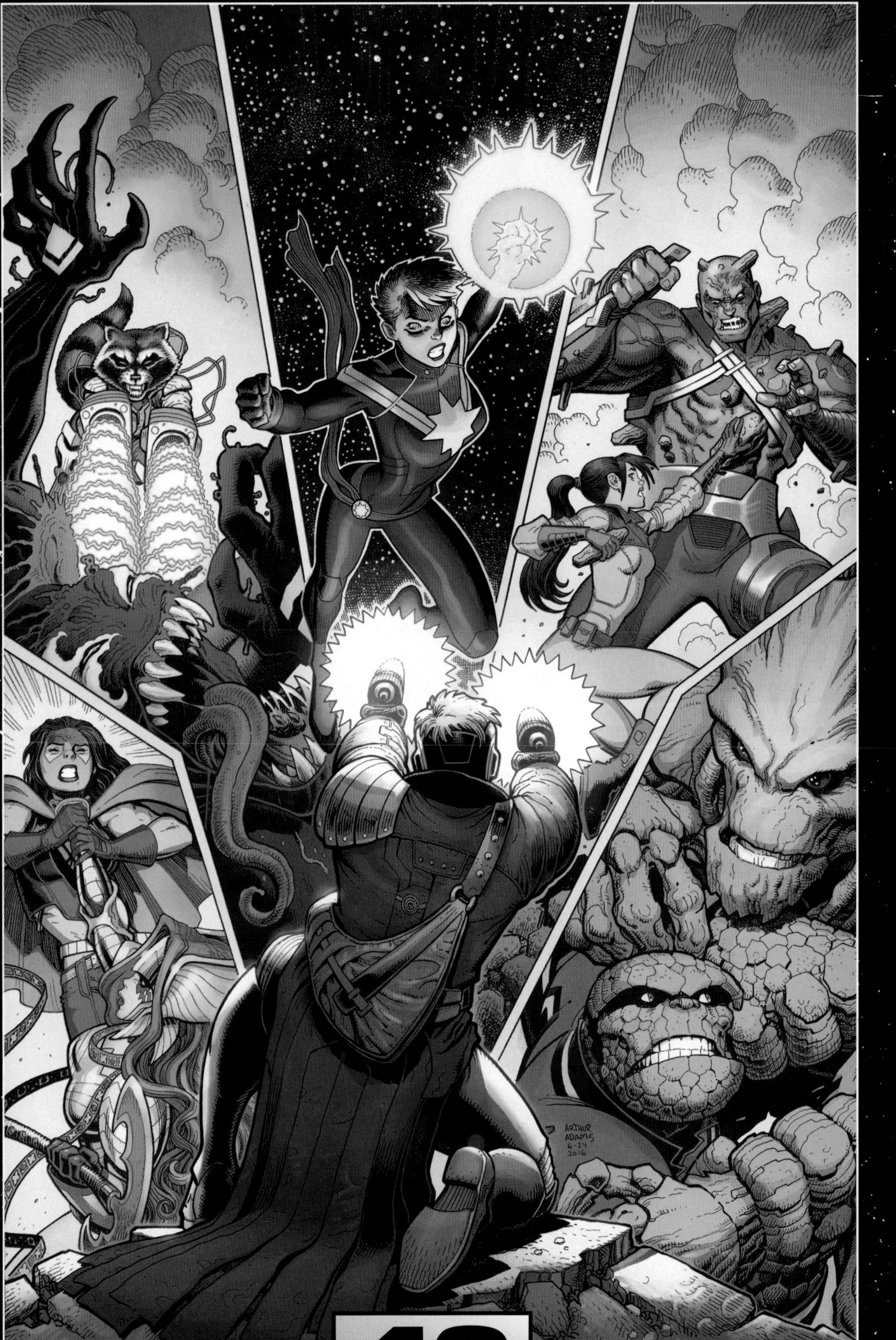
ARTHUR
ADAMS
6-24
2016

13

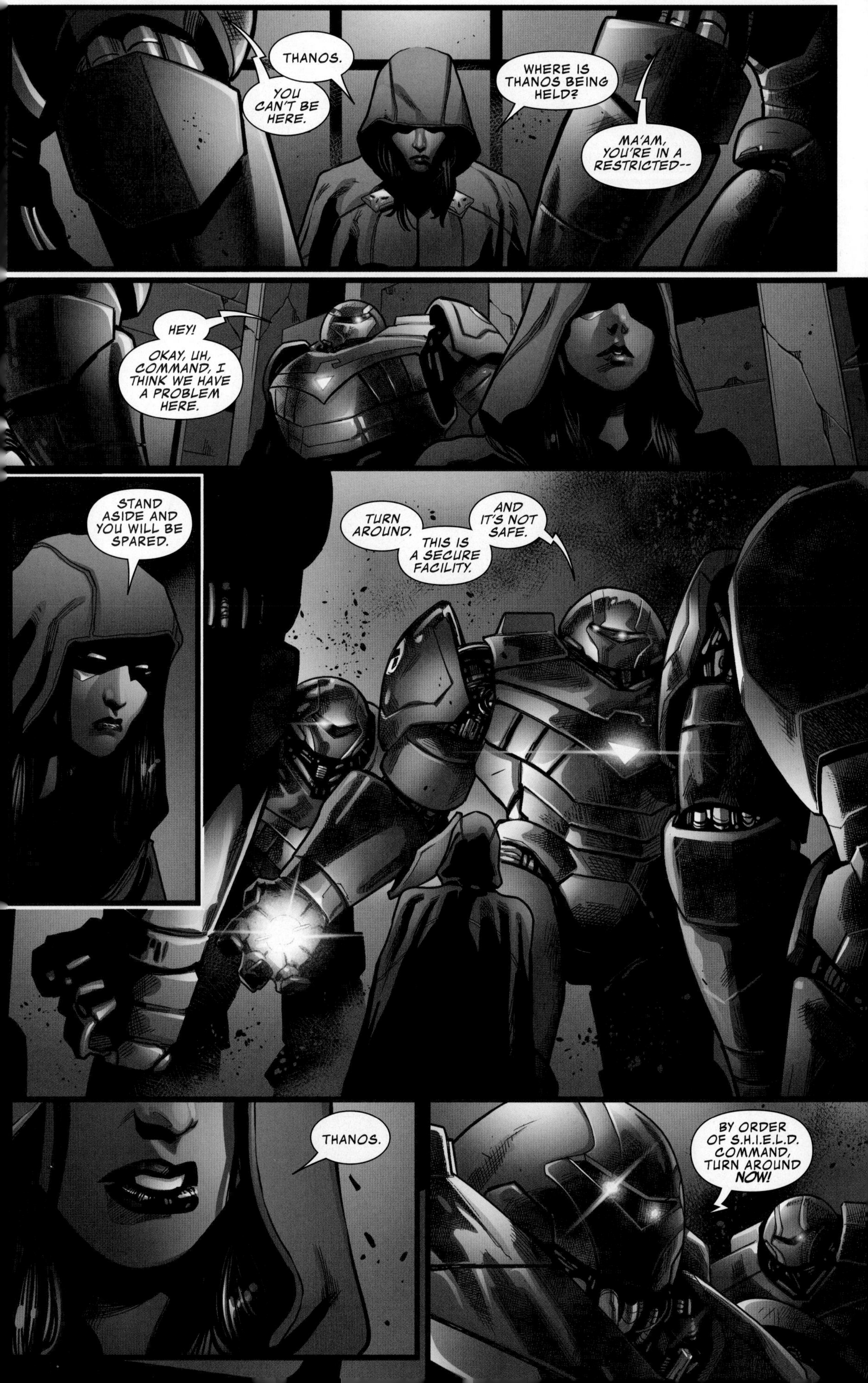
THANOS.
YOU CAN'T BE HERE.
WHERE IS THANOS BEING HELD?
MA'AM, YOU'RE IN A RESTRICTED--
HEY!
OKAY, UH, COMMAND, I THINK WE HAVE A PROBLEM HERE.
STAND ASIDE AND YOU WILL BE SPARED.
TURN AROUND.
THIS IS A SECURE FACILITY.
AND IT'S NOT SAFE.
THANOS.
BY ORDER OF S.H.I.E.L.D. COMMAND, TURN AROUND NOW!

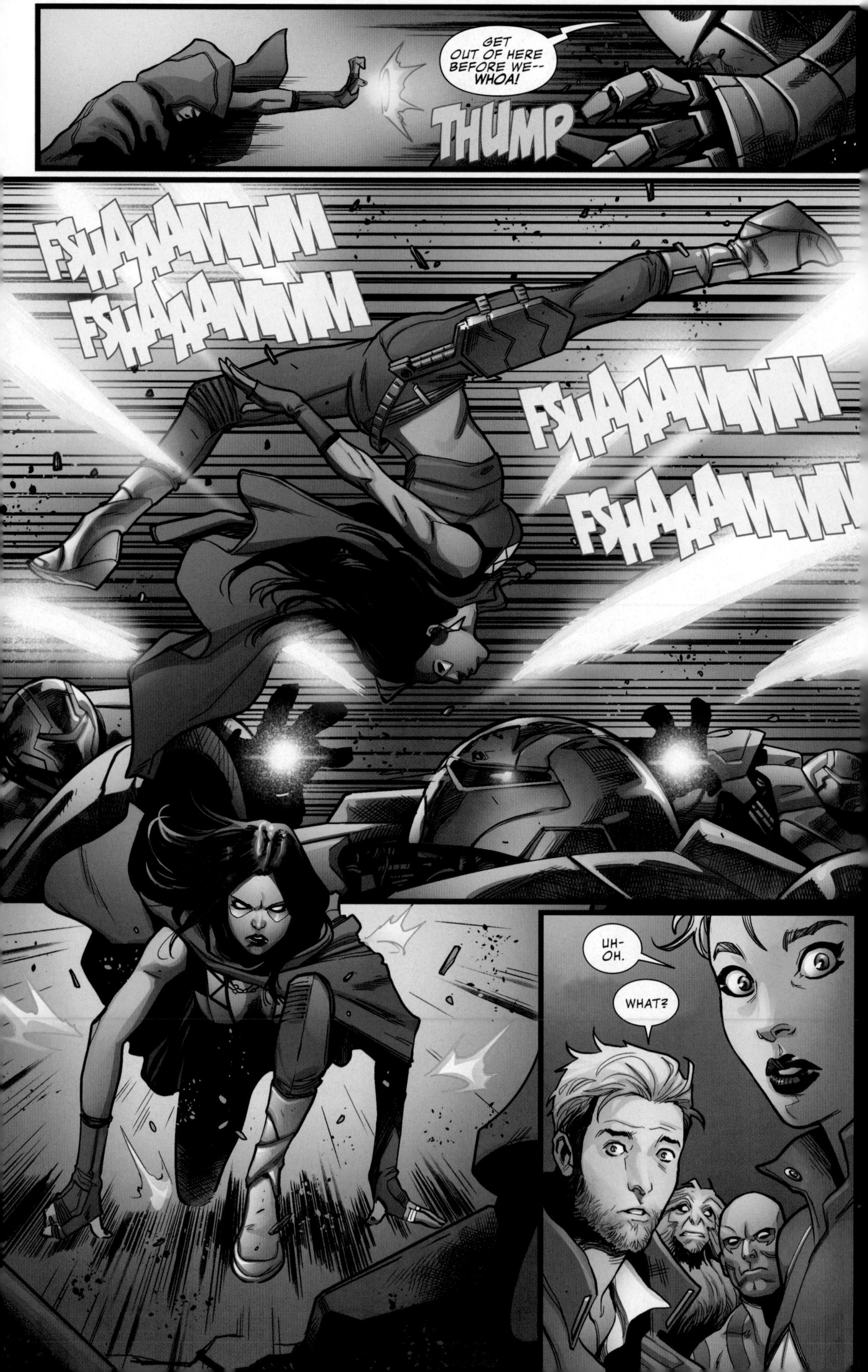
GET OUT OF HERE BEFORE WE-- WHOA!
THUMP
FSHAAAMMM
FSHAAAMMM
FSHAAAMMM
FSHAAAMMM
UH-OH.
WHAT?

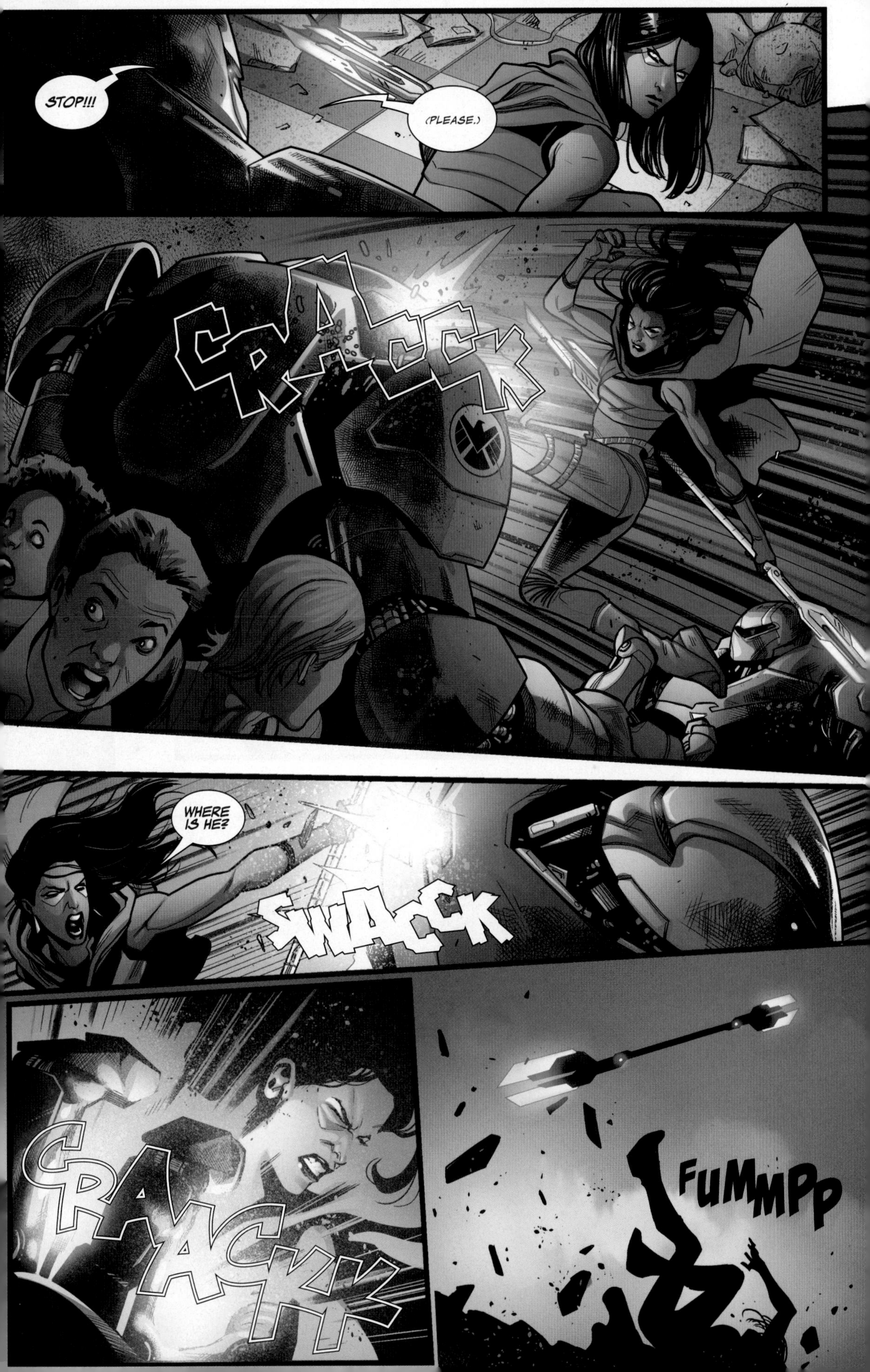
STOP!!!
(PLEASE.)
CRACCK
WHERE IS HE?
SWACCK
CRACKK
FUMMPP

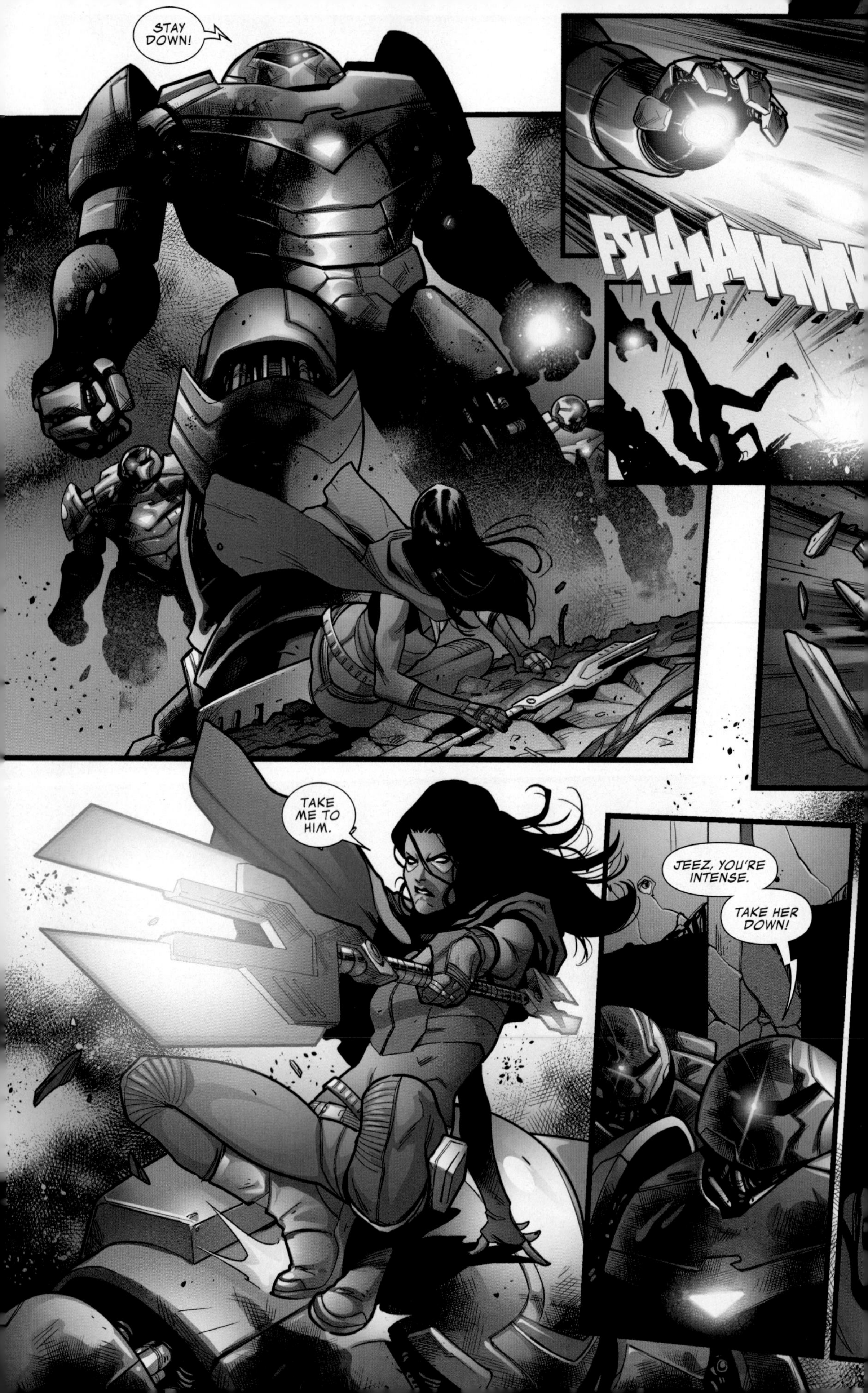
STAY DOWN!
FSHAAAAMMM
TAKE ME TO HIM.
JEEZ, YOU'RE INTENSE.
TAKE HER DOWN!

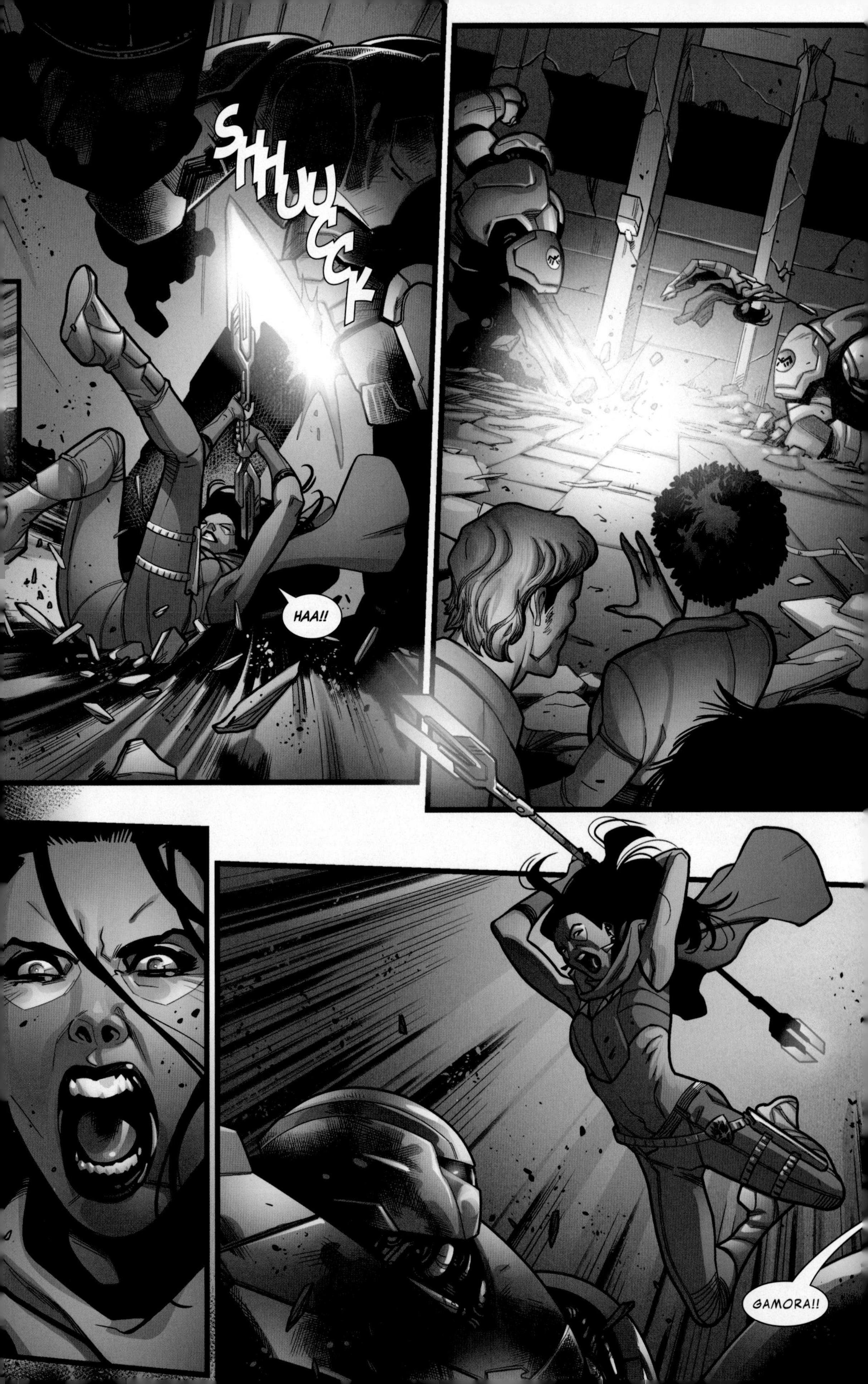
SHHUUCCK
HAA!!
GAMORA!!

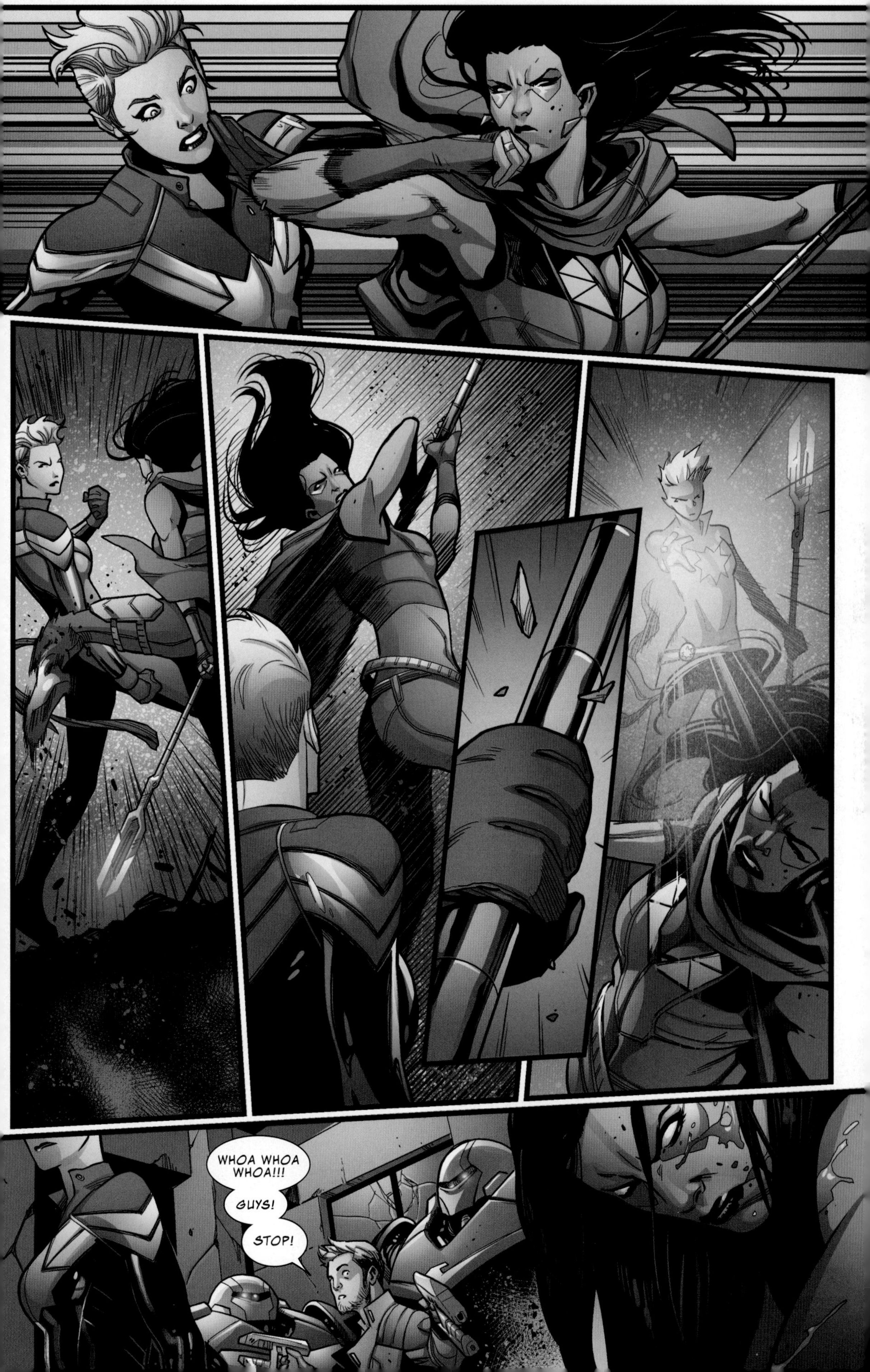
WHOA WHOA WHOA!!!
GUYS!
STOP!

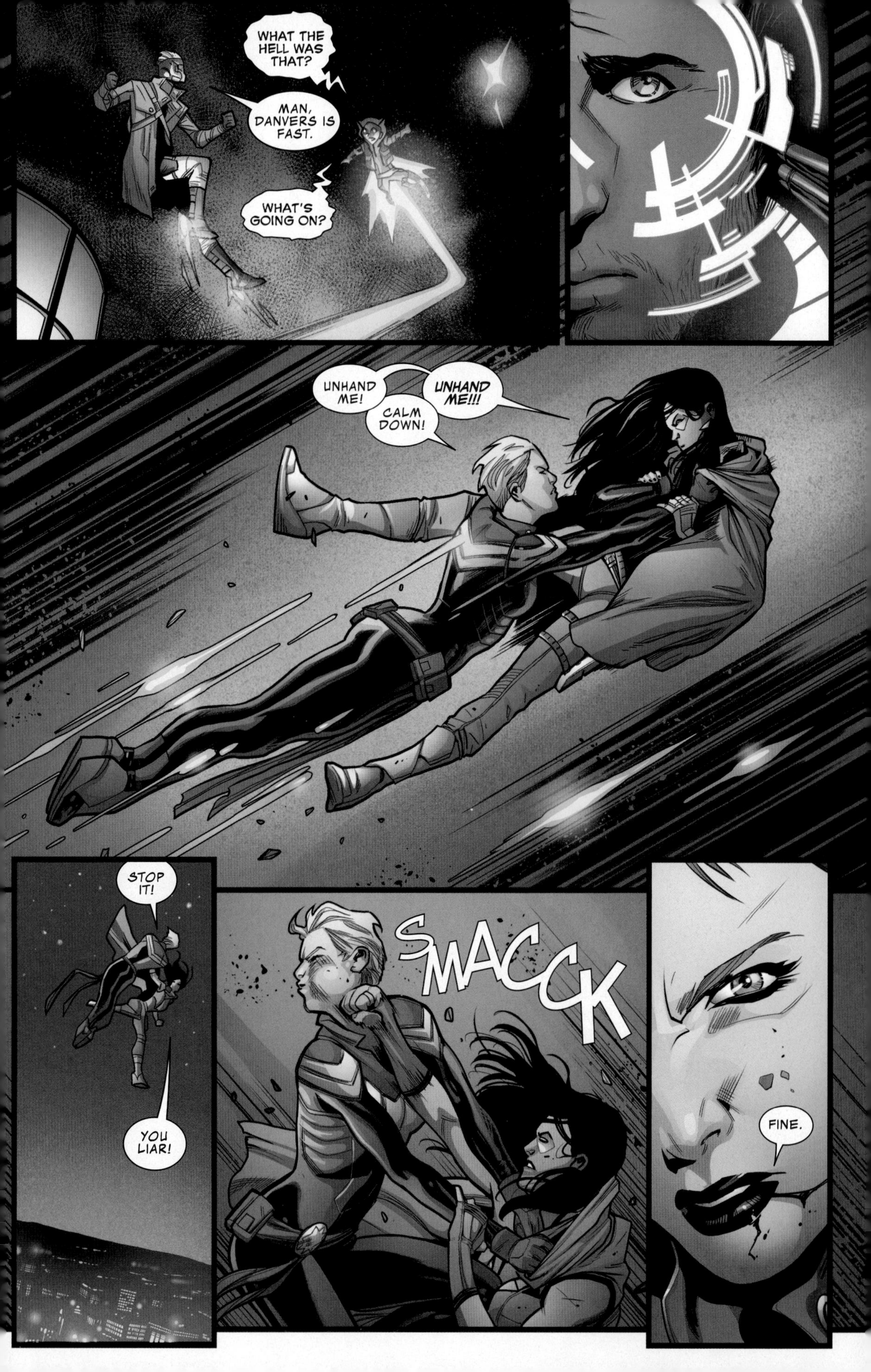
WHAT THE HELL WAS THAT?
MAN, DANVERS IS FAST.
WHAT'S GOING ON?
UNHAND ME!
CALM DOWN!
UNHAND ME!!!
STOP IT!
YOU LIAR!
SMACCK
FINE.

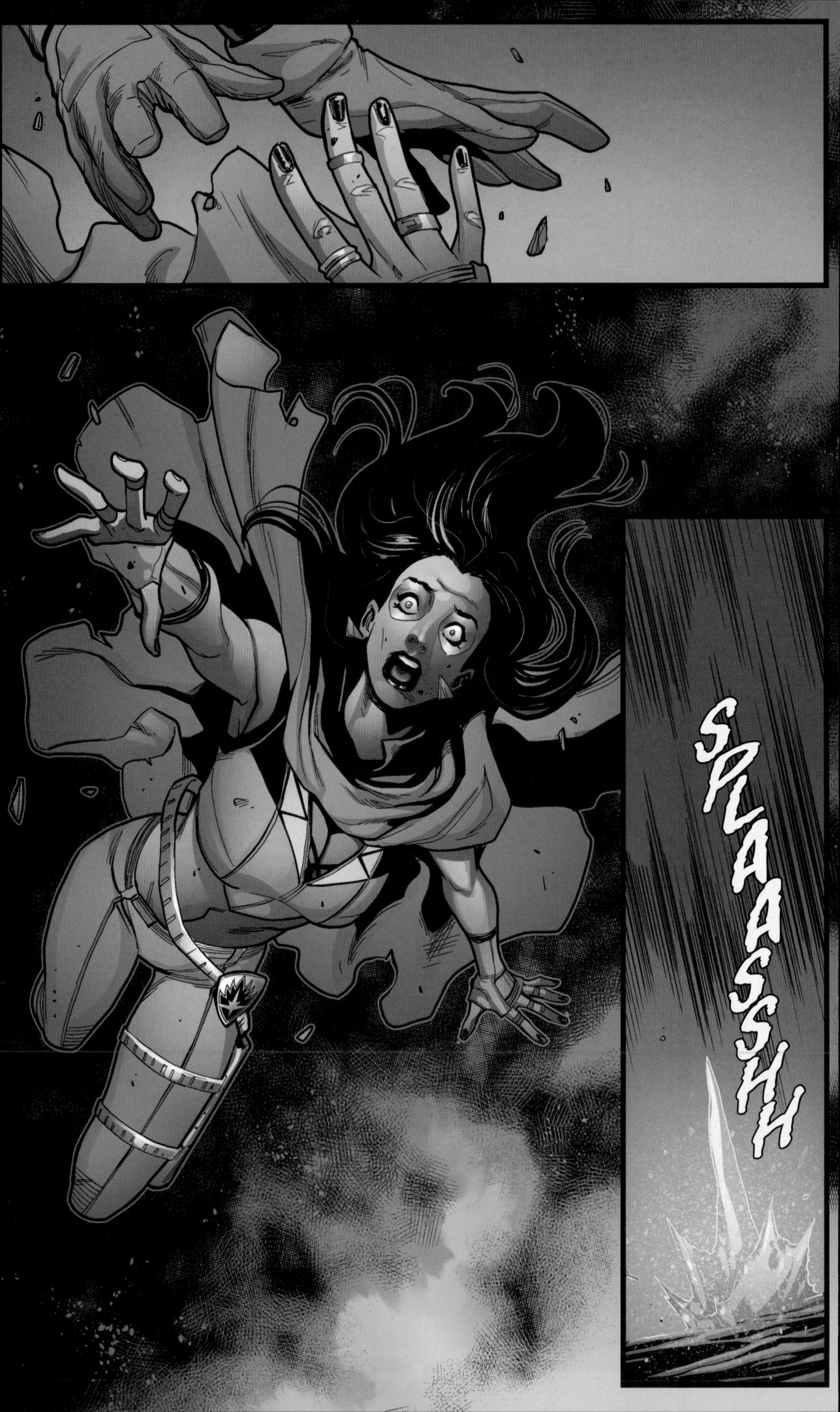
SPLAASSHH

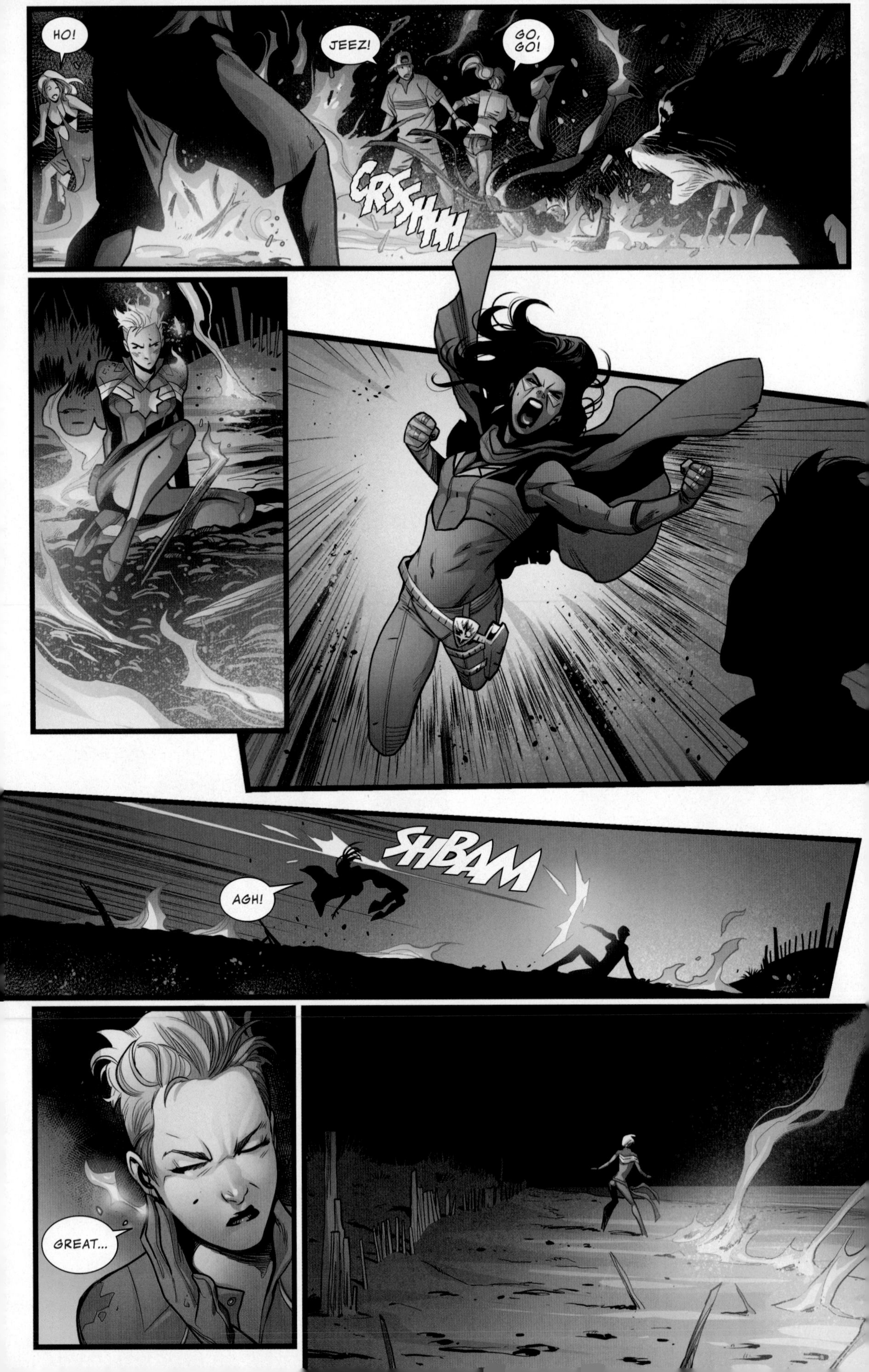
HO!
JEEZ!
GO, GO!
CRSSHHH
SHBAM
AGH!
GREAT...

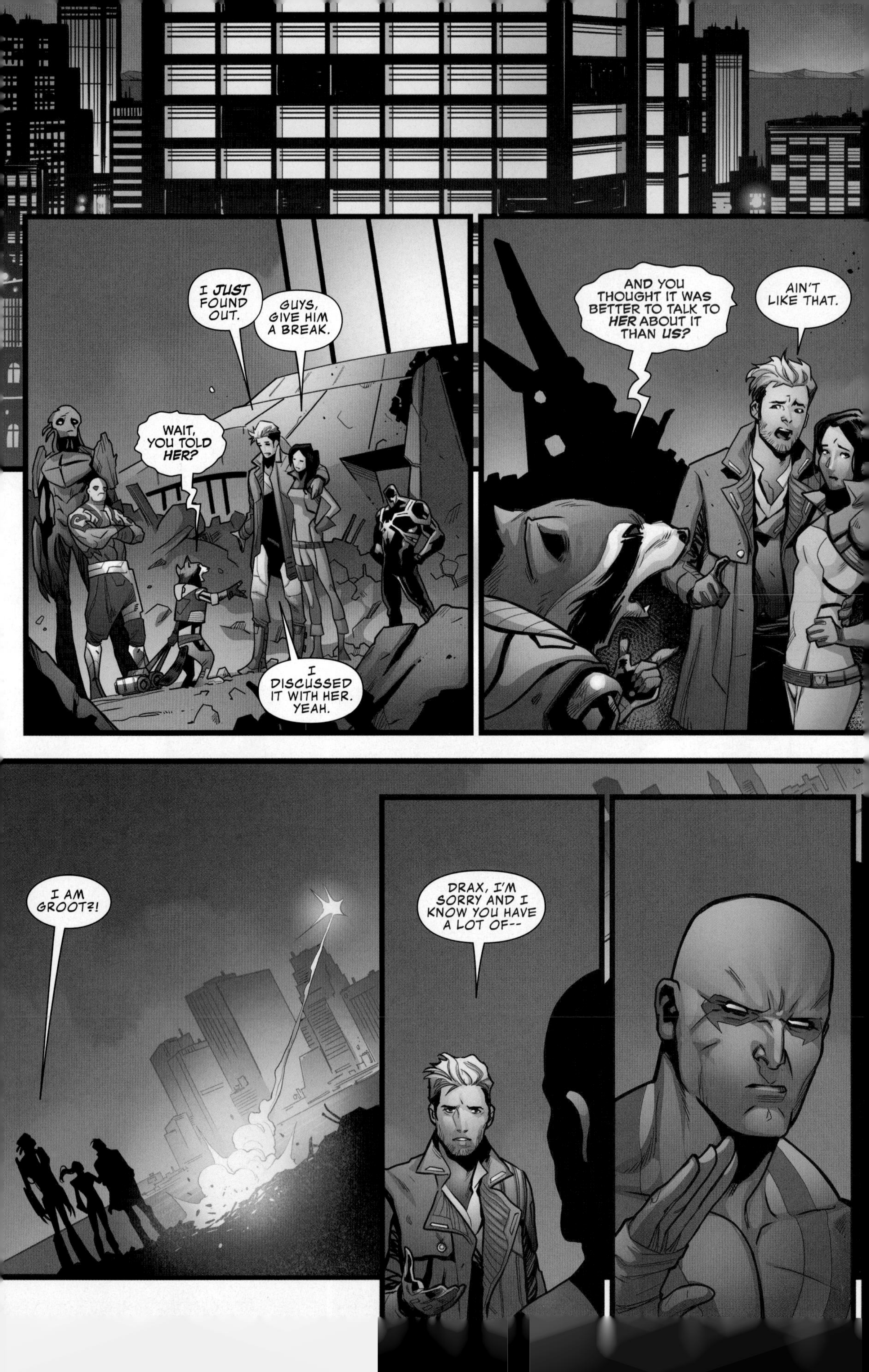
I JUST FOUND OUT.
GUYS, GIVE HIM A BREAK.
WAIT, YOU TOLD HER?
I DISCUSSED IT WITH HER. YEAH.
AND YOU THOUGHT IT WAS BETTER TO TALK TO HER ABOUT IT THAN US?
AIN'T LIKE THAT.
I AM GROOT?!
DRAX, I'M SORRY AND I KNOW YOU HAVE A LOT OF--

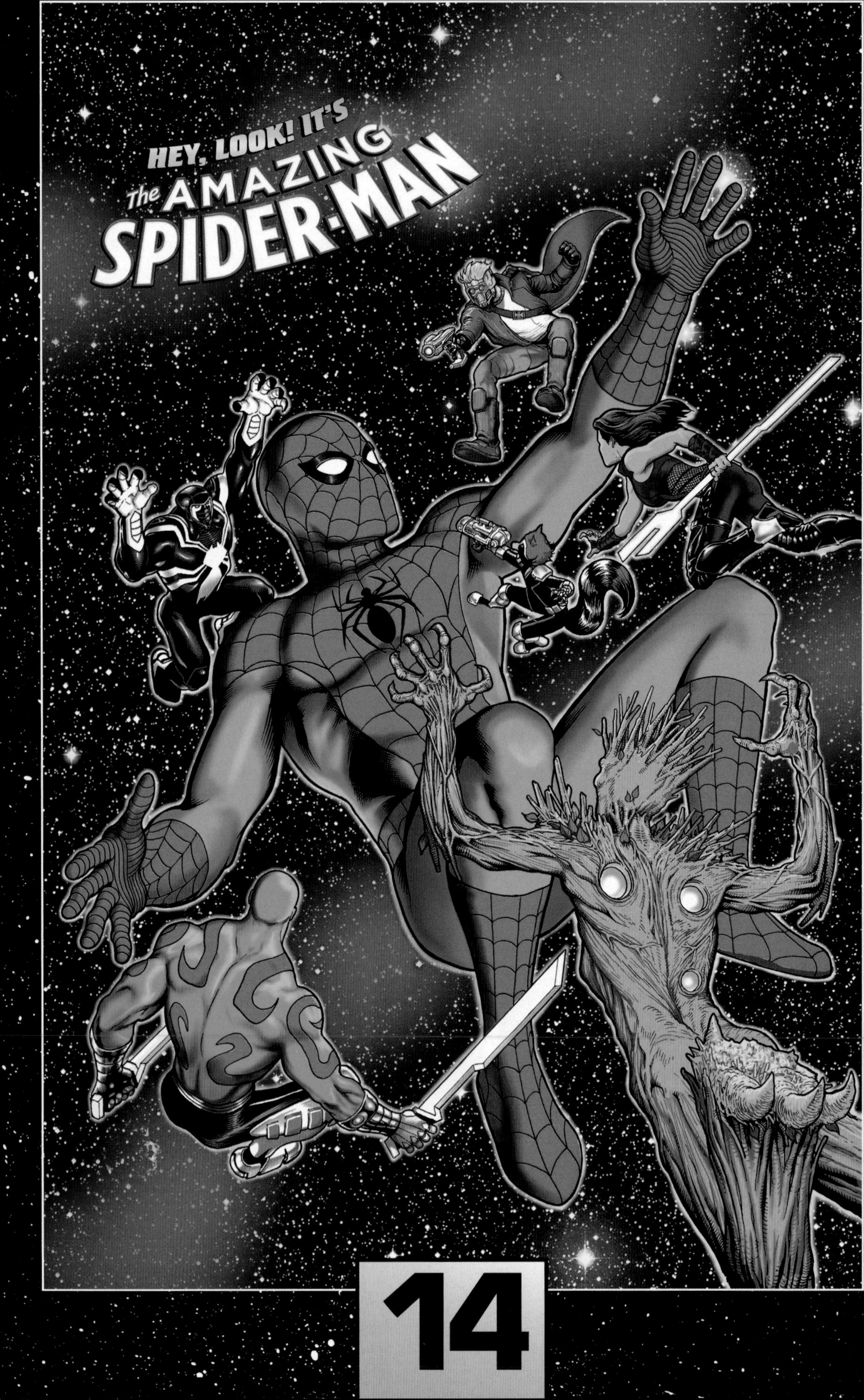
HEY, LOOK! IT'S
The AMAZING
SPIDER-MAN
14

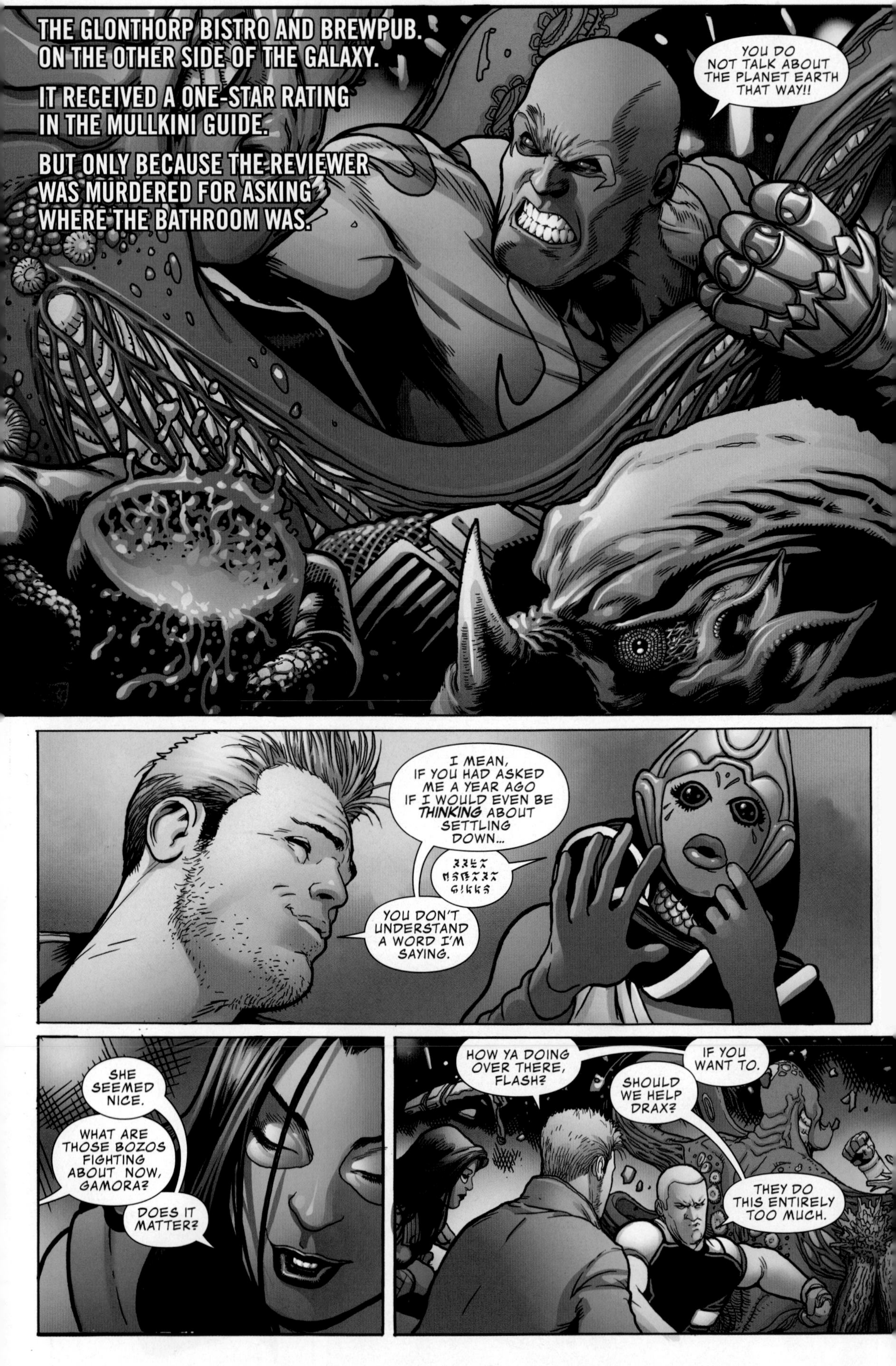
THE GLONTHORP BISTRO AND BREWPUB. ON THE OTHER SIDE OF THE GALAXY.
IT RECEIVED A ONE-STAR RATING IN THE MULLKINI GUIDE.
BUT ONLY BECAUSE THE REVIEWER WAS MURDERED FOR ASKING WHERE THE BATHROOM WAS.
YOU DO NOT TALK ABOUT THE PLANET EARTH THAT WAY!!
I MEAN, IF YOU HAD ASKED ME A YEAR AGO IF I WOULD EVEN BE THINKING ABOUT SETTLING DOWN...
YOU DON'T UNDERSTAND A WORD I'M SAYING.
SHE SEEMED NICE.
WHAT ARE THOSE BOZOS FIGHTING ABOUT NOW, GAMORA?
DOES IT MATTER?
HOW YA DOING OVER THERE, FLASH?
IF YOU WANT TO.
SHOULD WE HELP DRAX?
THEY DO THIS ENTIRELY TOO MUCH.

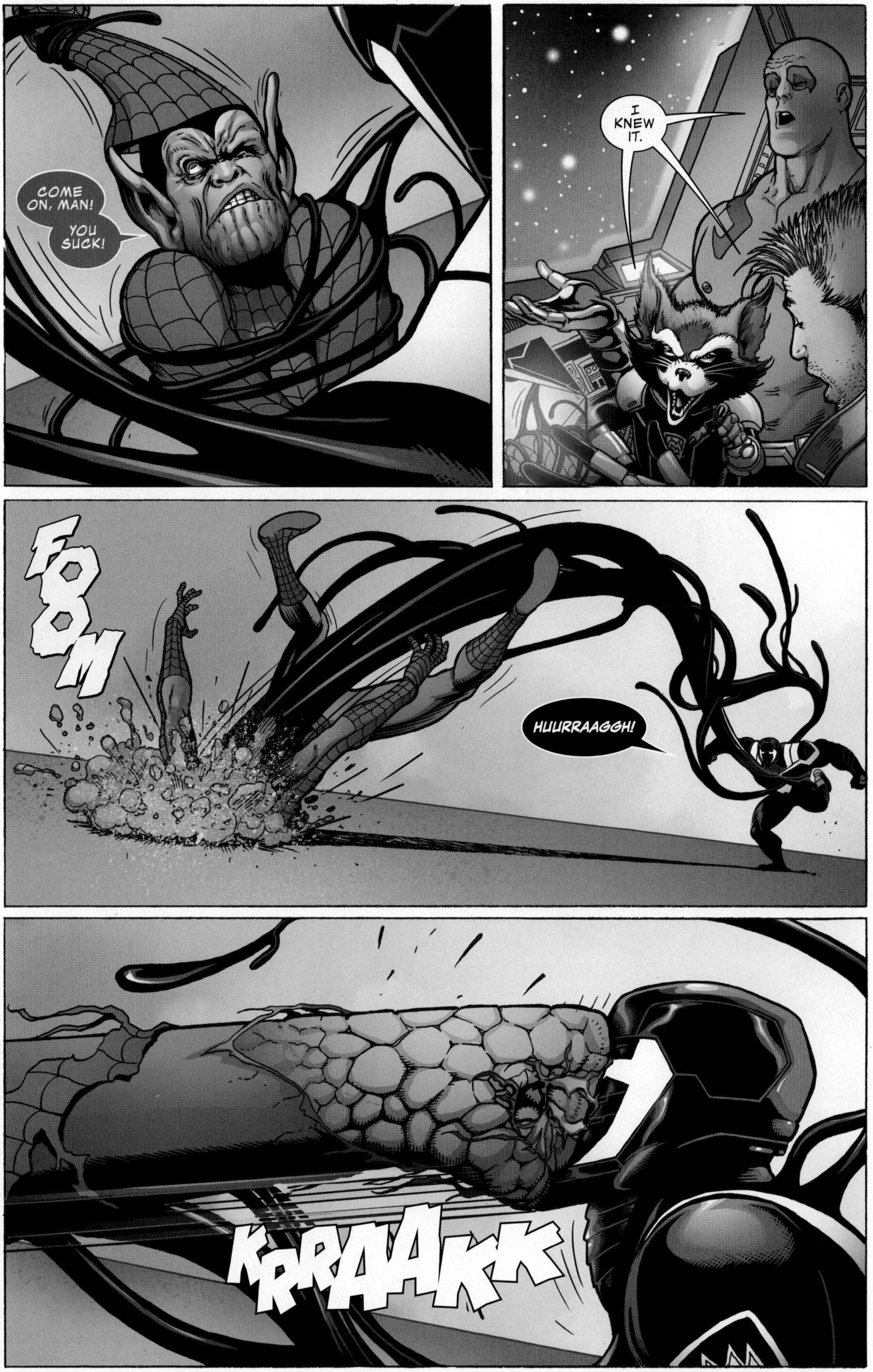
COME ON, MAN!
YOU SUCK!
I KNEW IT.
FOOM
HUURRAAGGH!
KRRAAKK

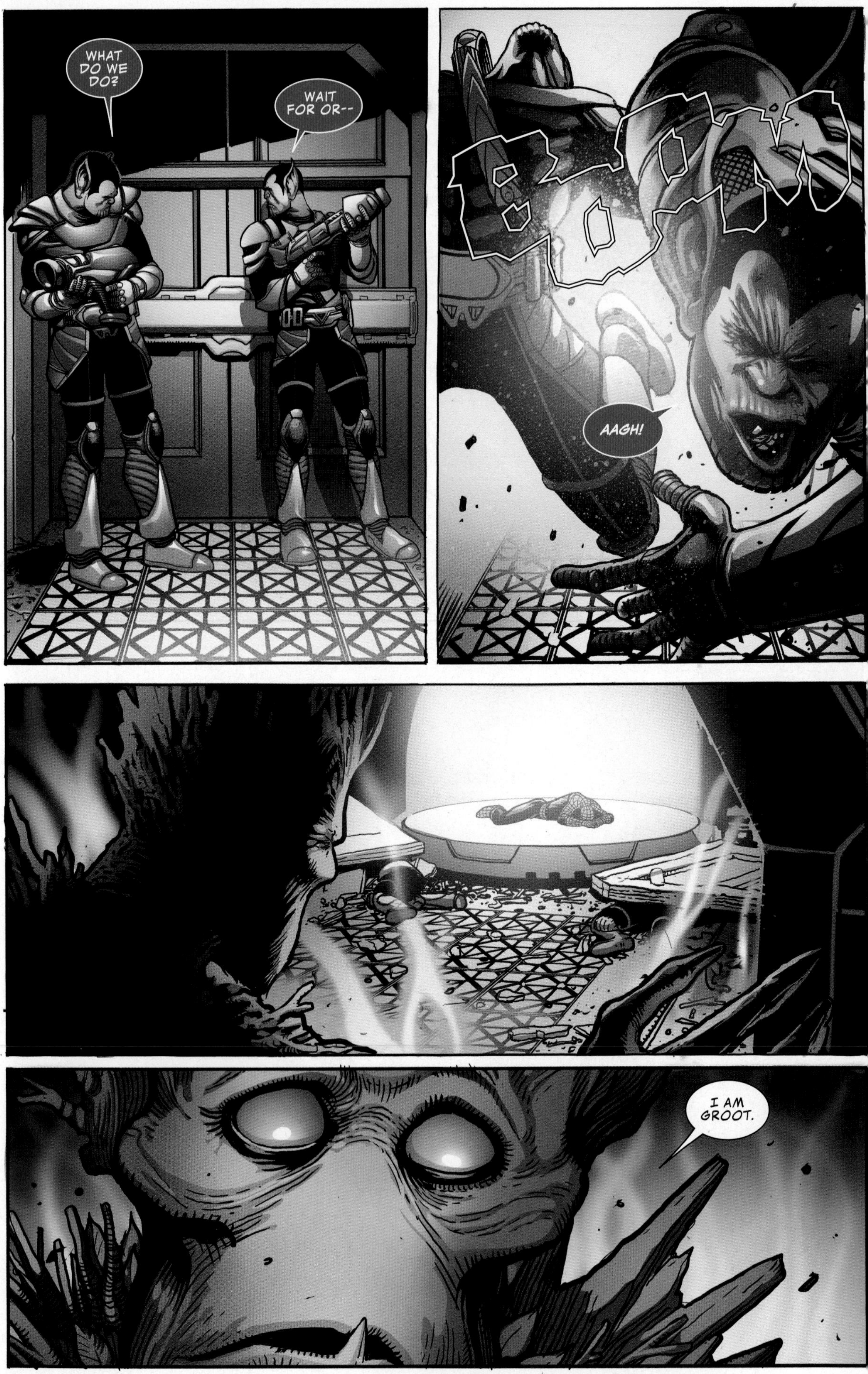

WHAT DO WE DO?
WAIT FOR OR--
BOOM
AAGH!
I AM GROOT.

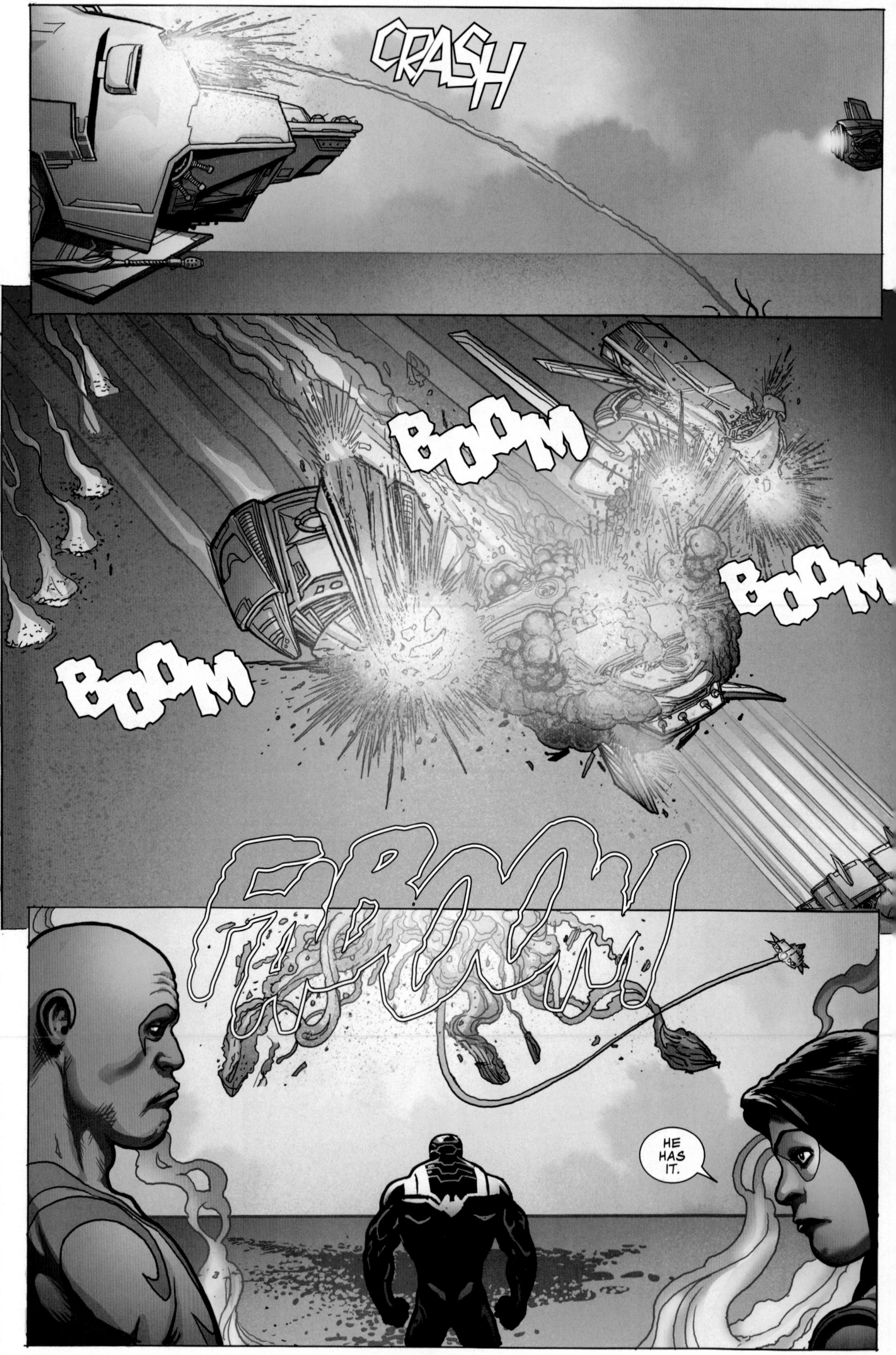
CRASH
BOOM
BOOM
BOOM
HE HAS IT.

NEXT: GROUNDED

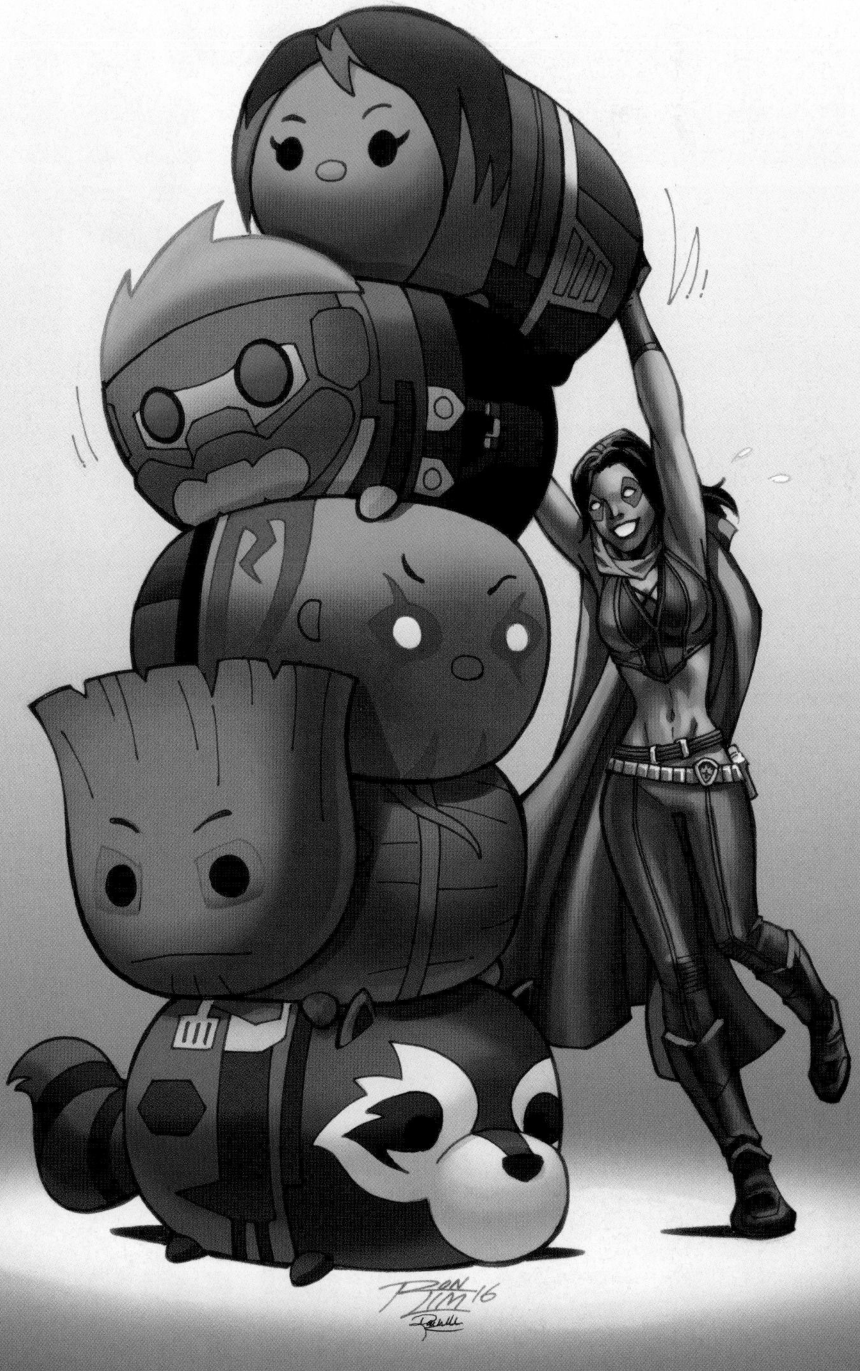

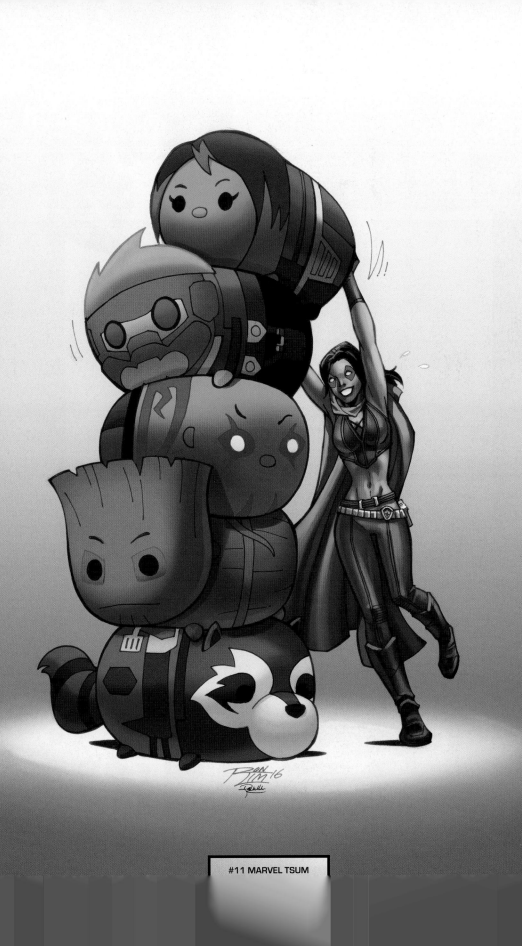

#11 MARVEL TSUM

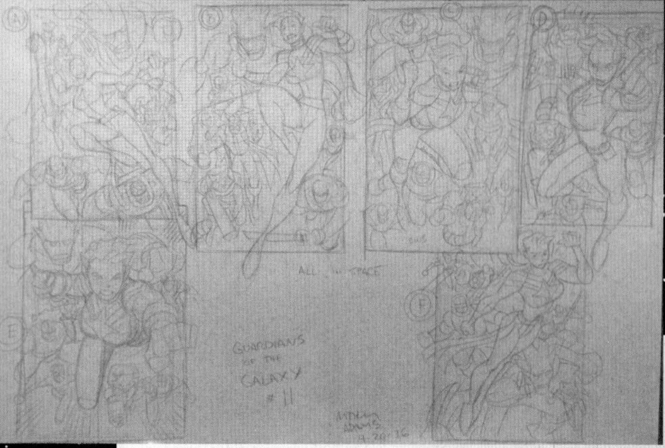
ALL IN SPACE
GUARDIANS OF THE GALAXY #11

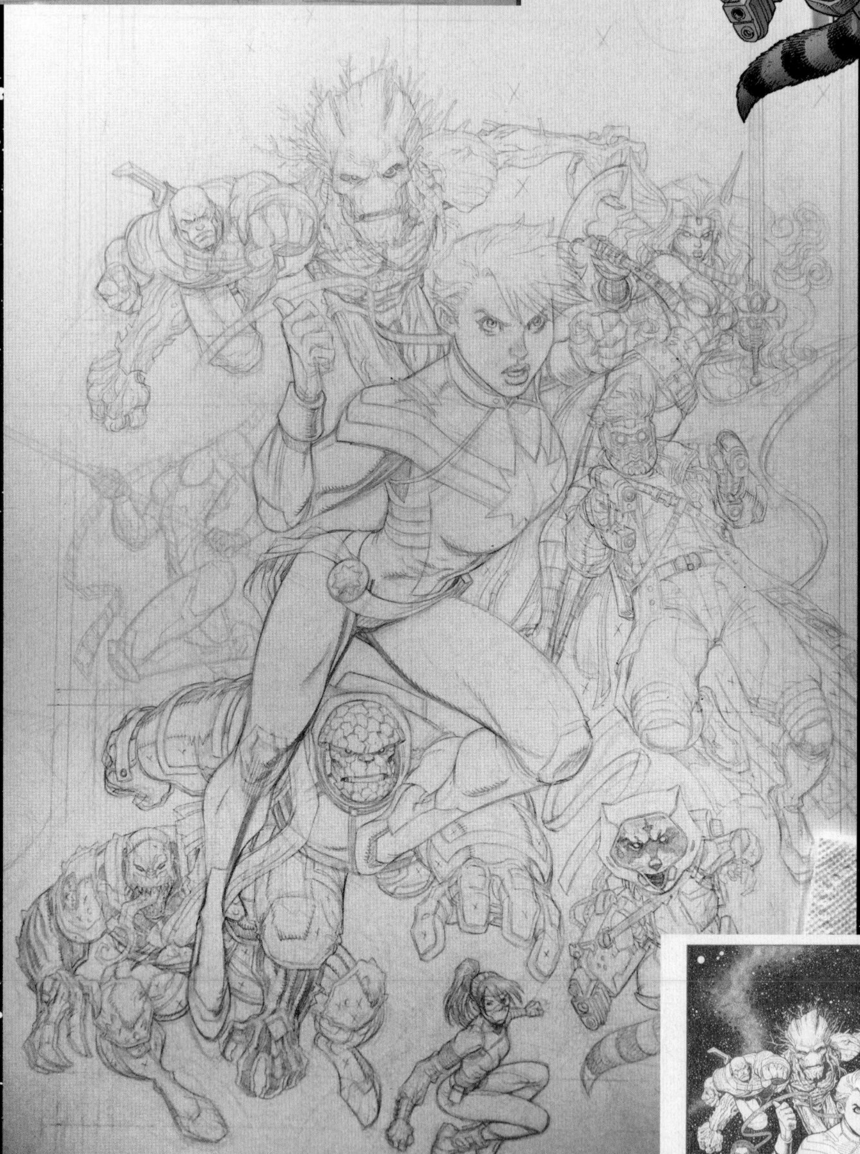

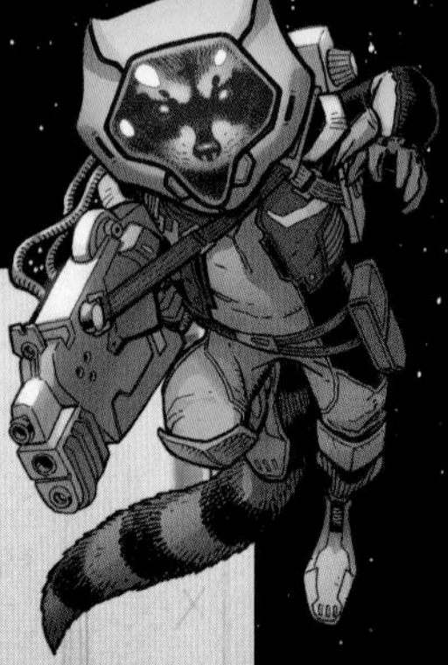

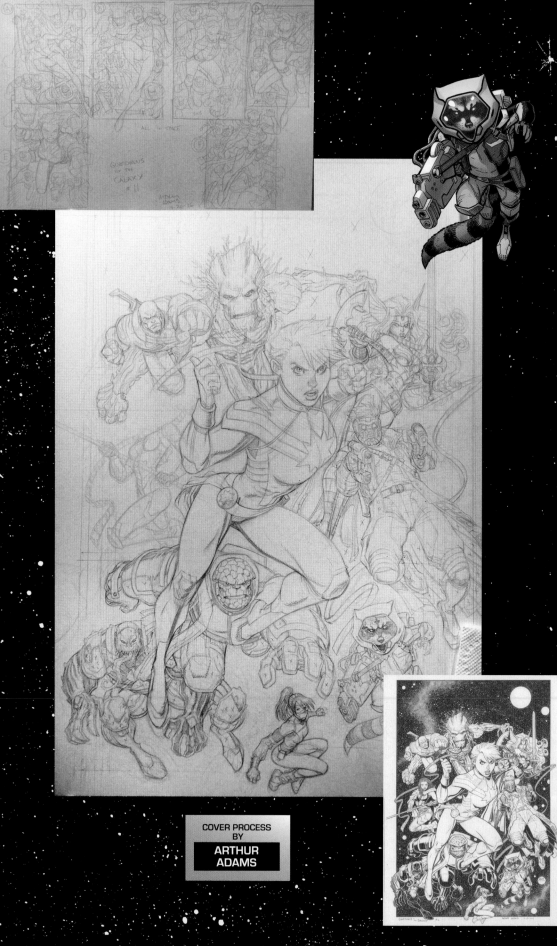

COVER PROCESS BY

ARTHUR ADAMS

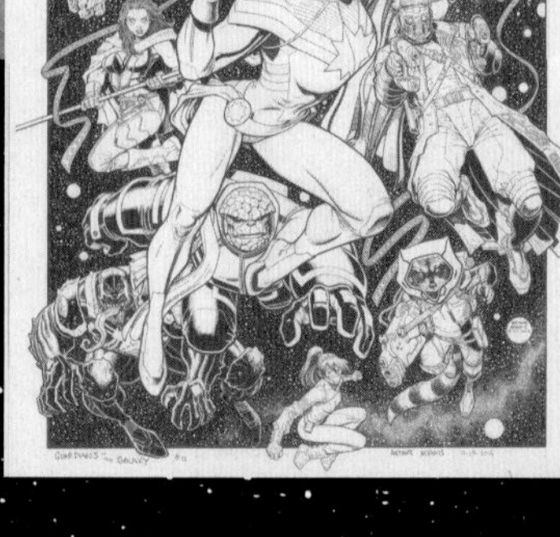

#11, PAGE 8 ART PROCESS BY
VALERIO SCHITI

#11, PAGE 11 ART PROCESS BY
VALERIO SCHITI

#11, PAGE 12 ART PROCESS BY
VALERIO SCHITI

#11, PAGE 13 ART PROCESS BY
VALERIO SCHITI

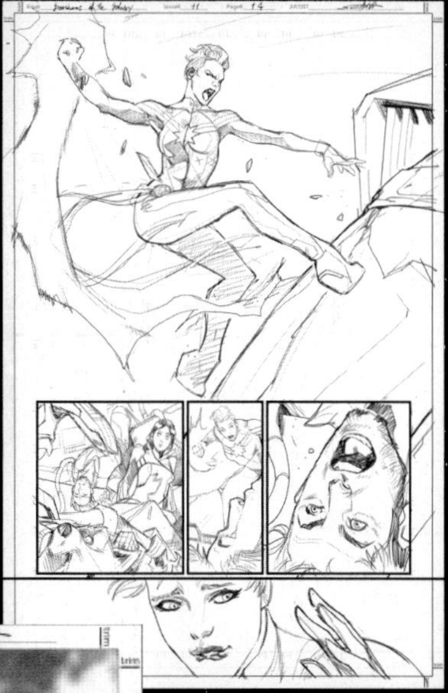

#11, PAGE 14 ART PROCESS BY

VALERIO SCHITI

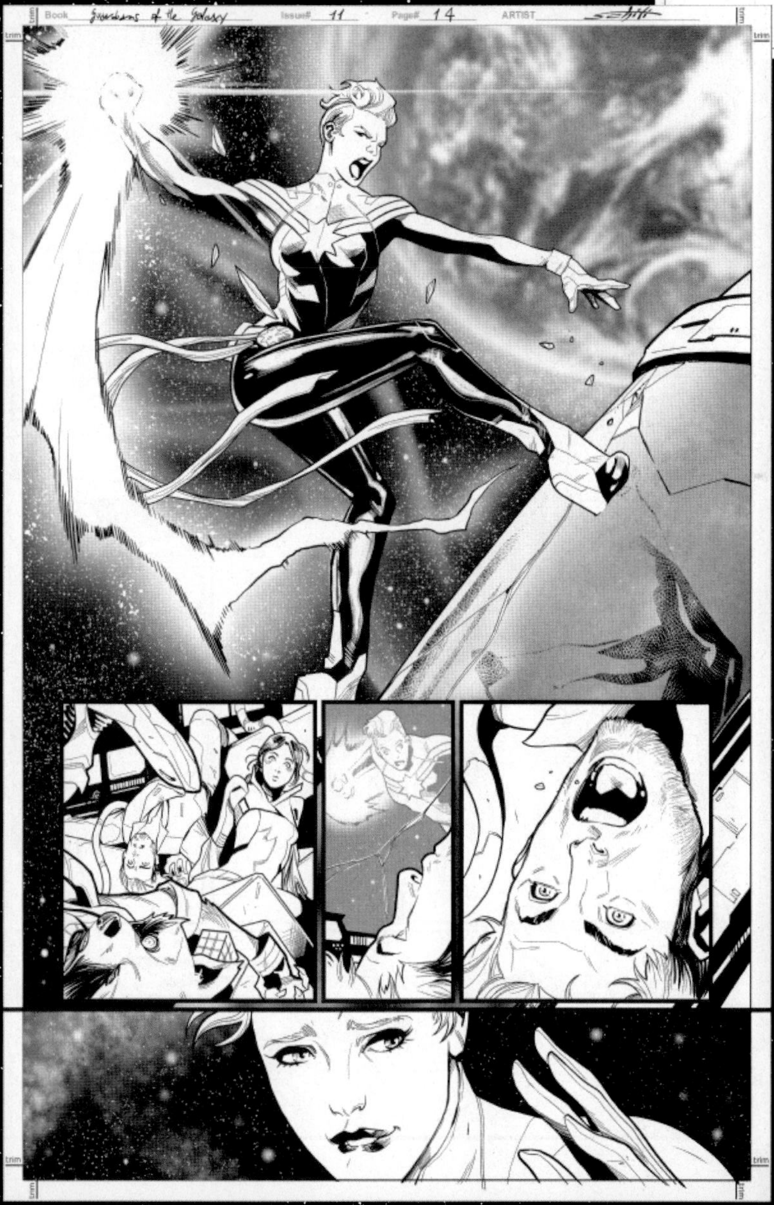

Book
Issue# 11
Page# 14
ARTIST
trim

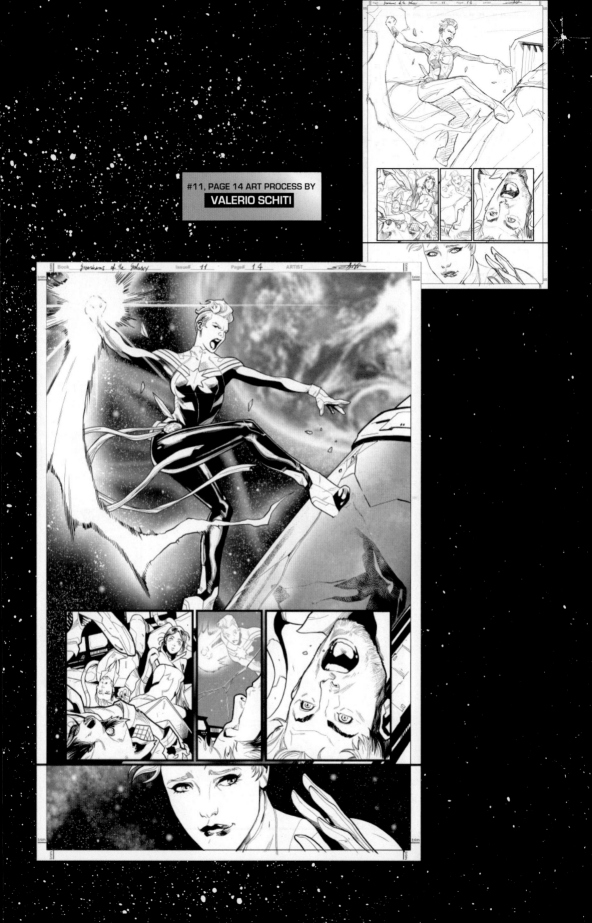

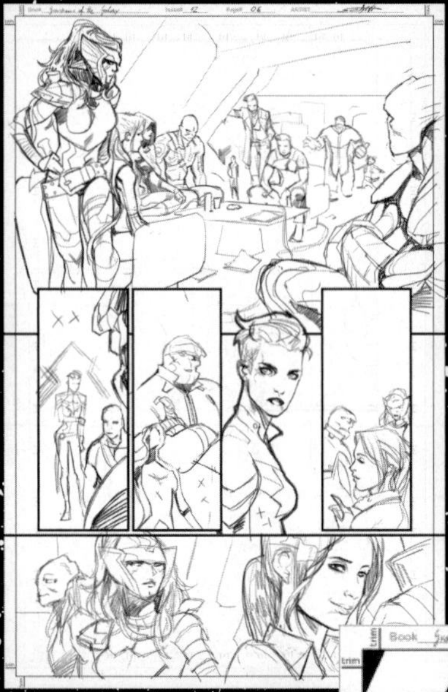

#12, PAGE 5 ART PROCESS BY
VALERIO SCHITI

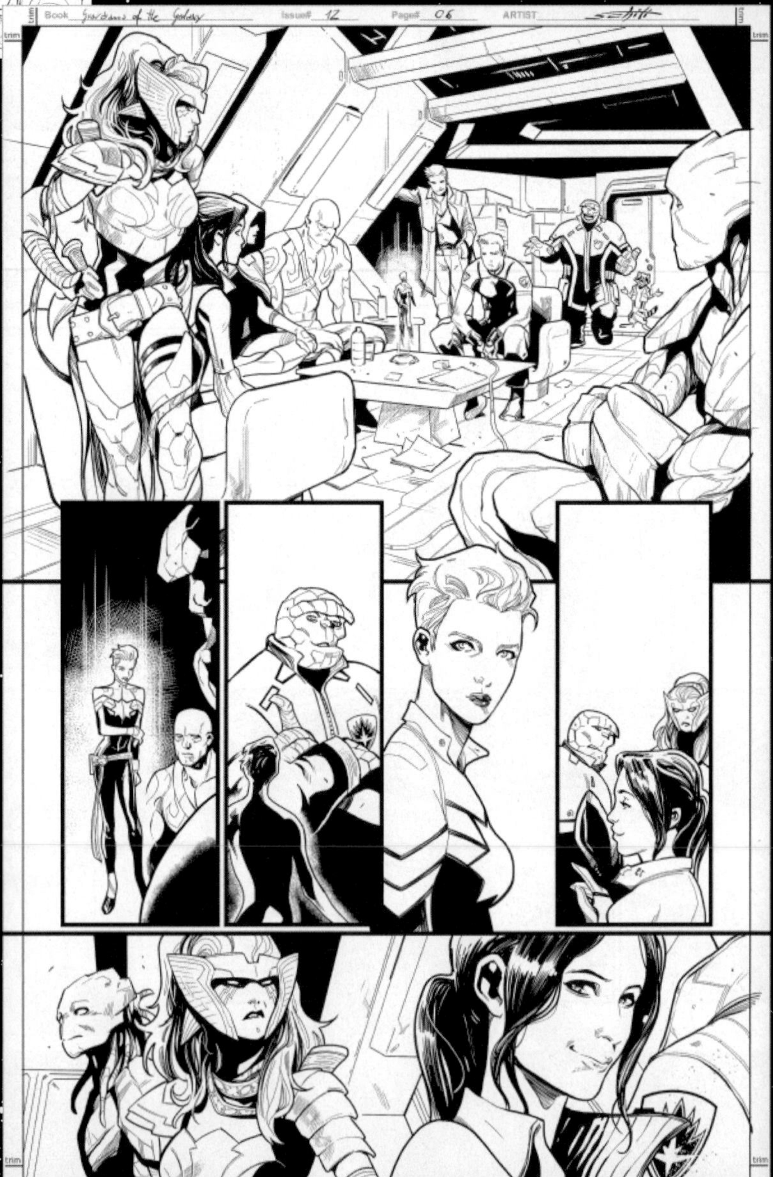
Book Guardians of the Galaxy Issue# 12 Page# 06 ARTIST

#12, PAGE 6 ART PROCESS BY
VALERIO SCHITI

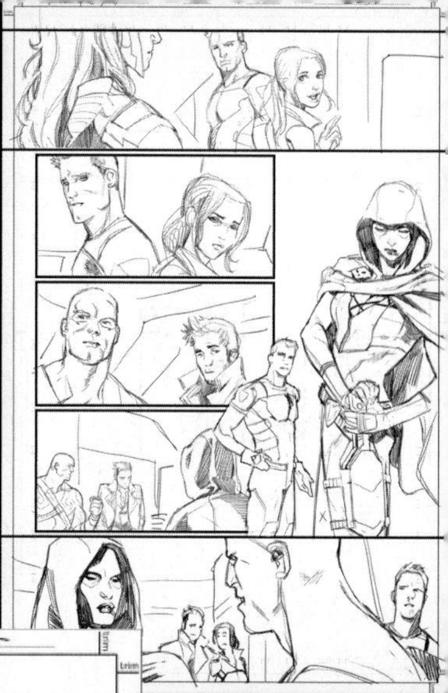

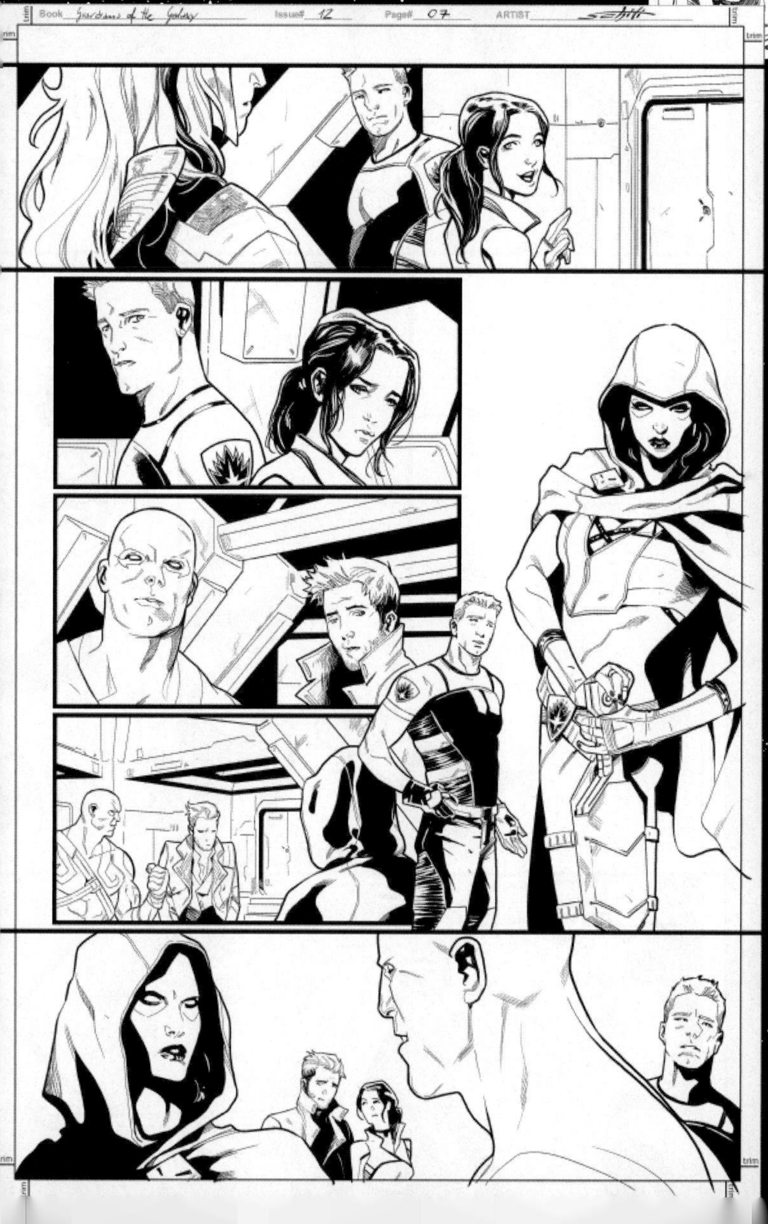
Book Guardians of the Galaxy
Issue# 12
Page# 07
ARTIST

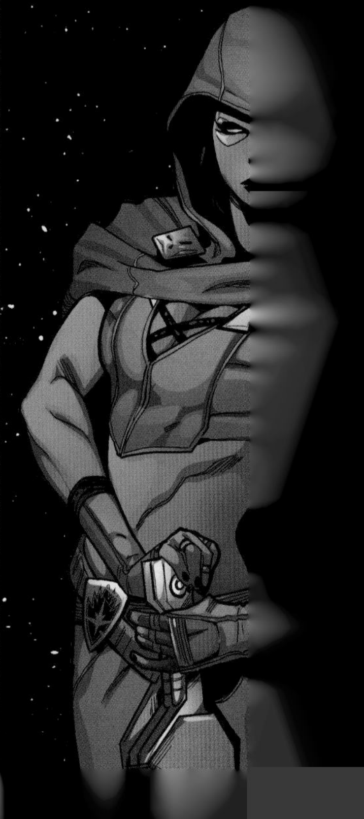

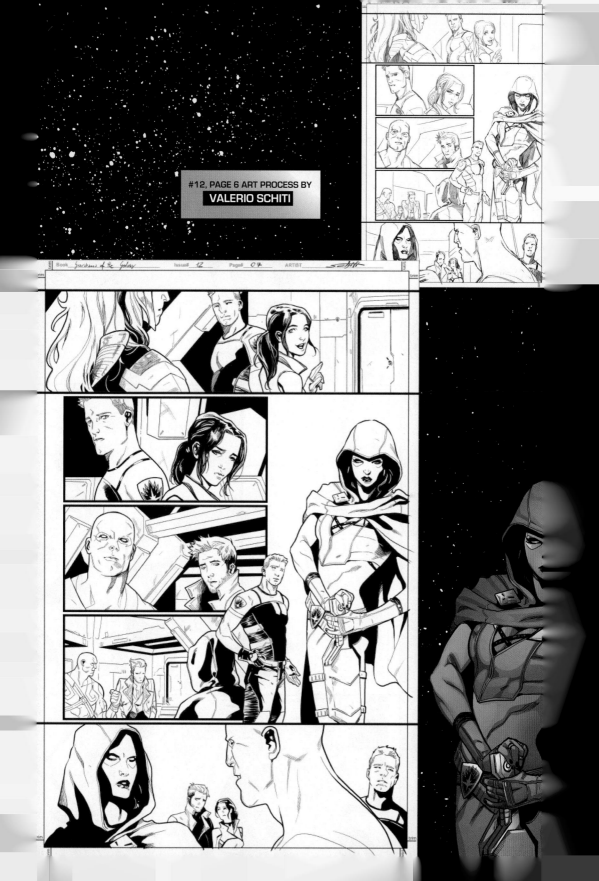

Book Guardians of the Galaxy   Issue# 12   Page# 08-09   ARTIST

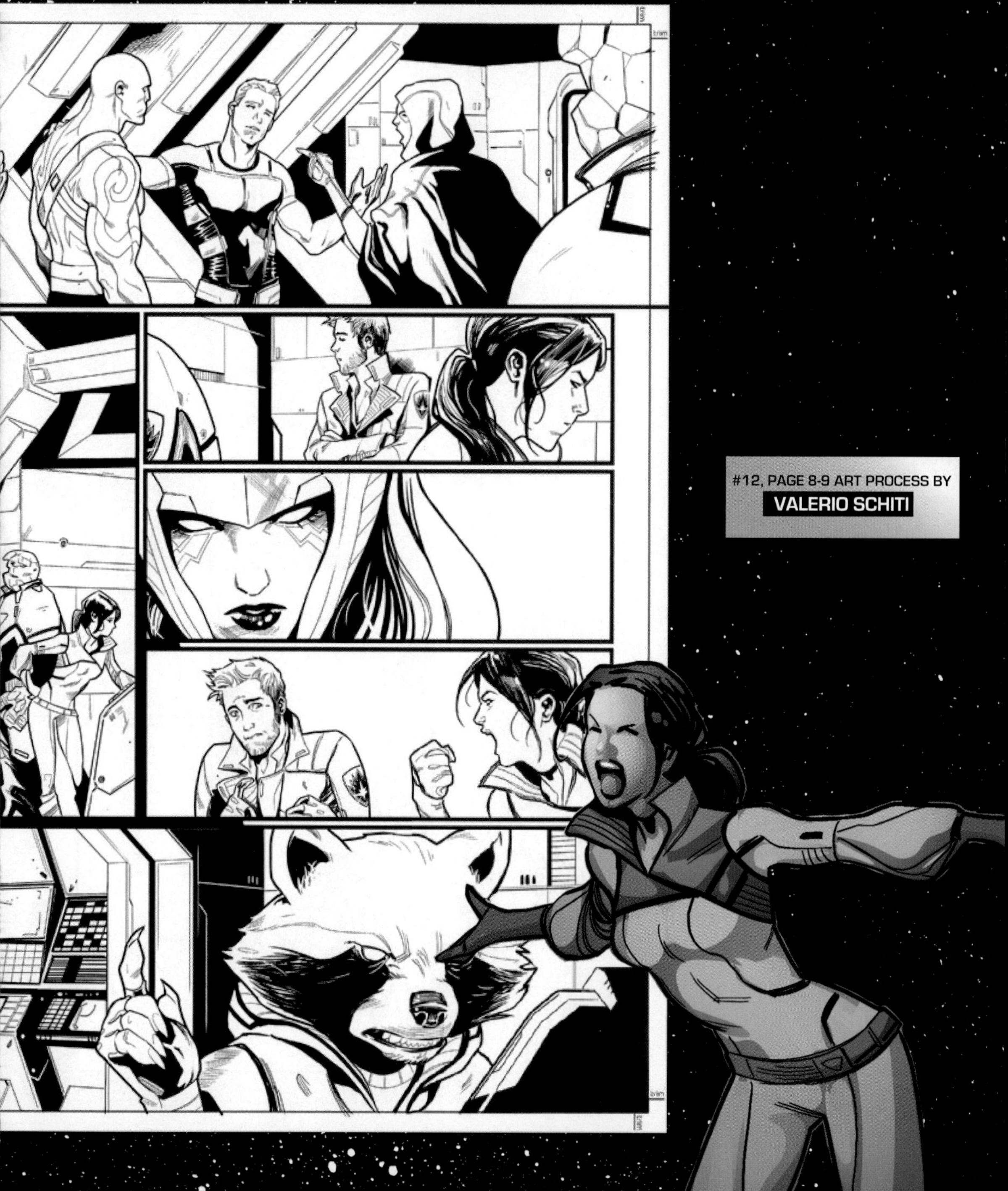
trim
trim
trim
trim

#12, PAGE 8-9 ART PROCESS BY
VALERIO SCHITI

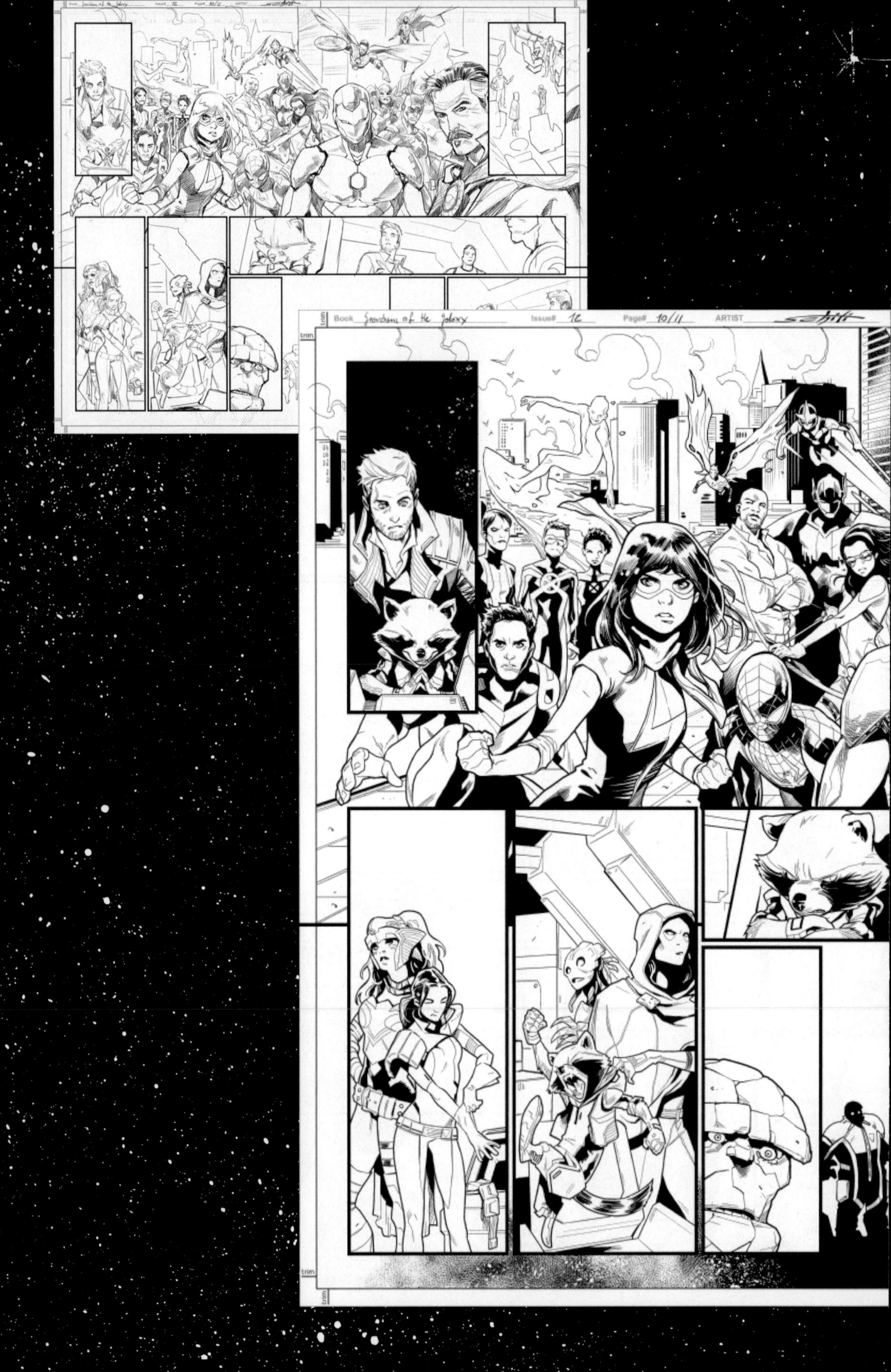

Book Guardians of the Galaxy
Issue# 12
Page# 10/11
ARTIST
trim

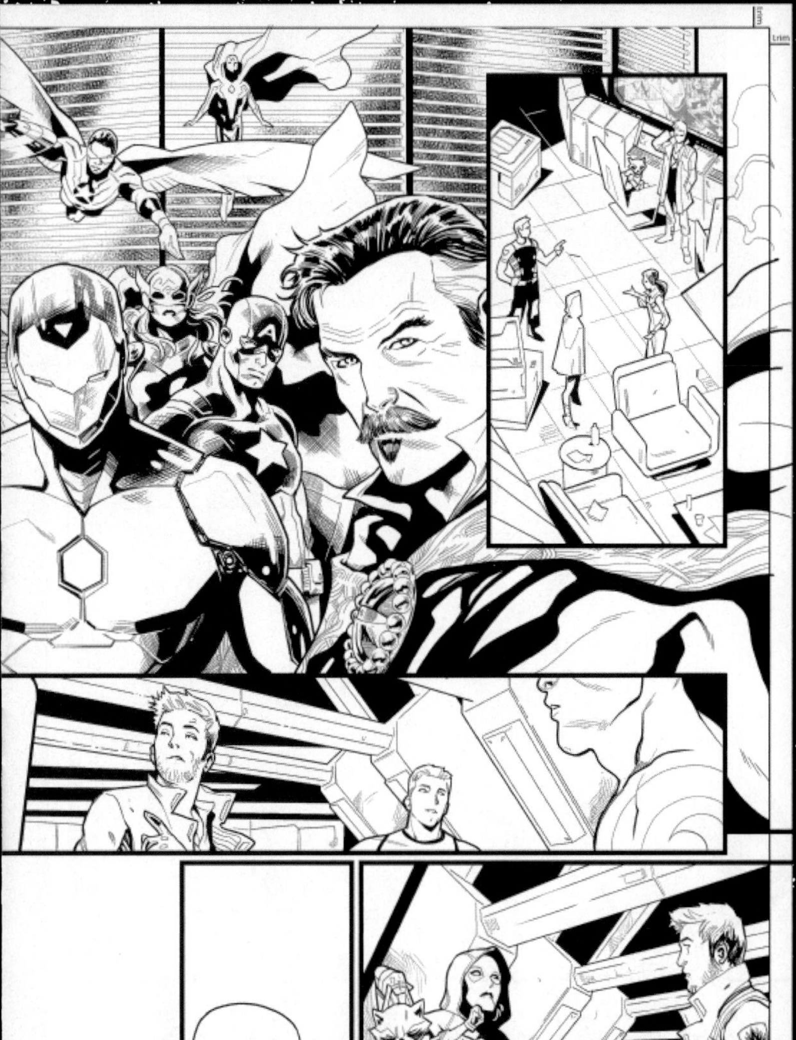

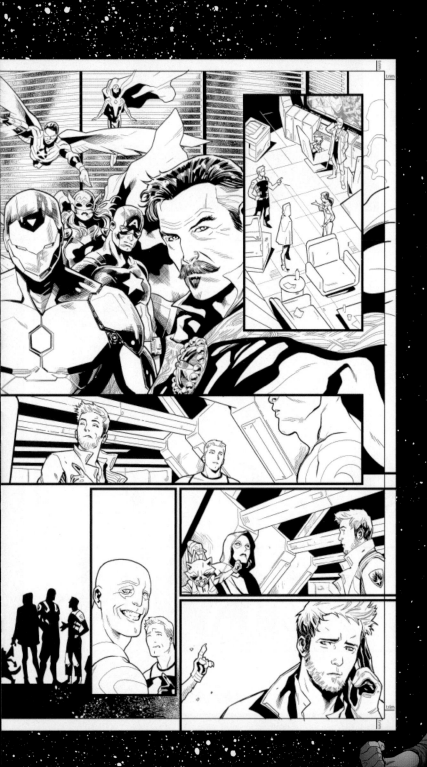

#12, PAGE 10-11 ART PROCESS
VALERIO SCHITI

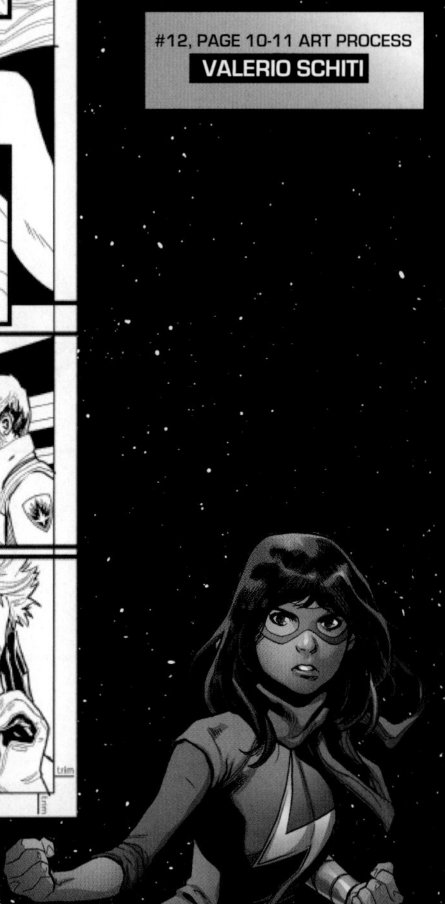

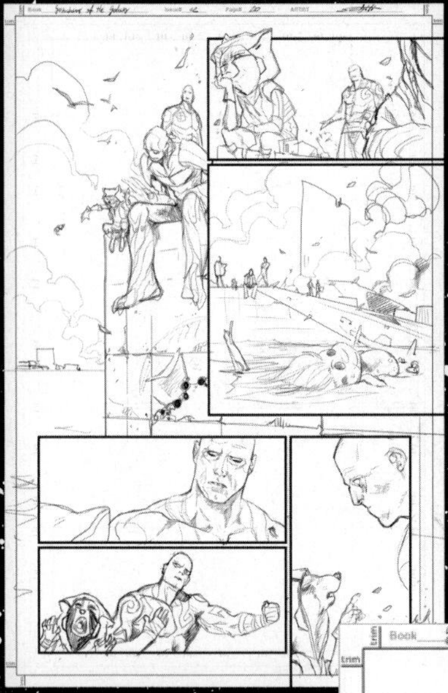

#12, PAGE 21 ART PROCESS BY

VALERIO SCHITI

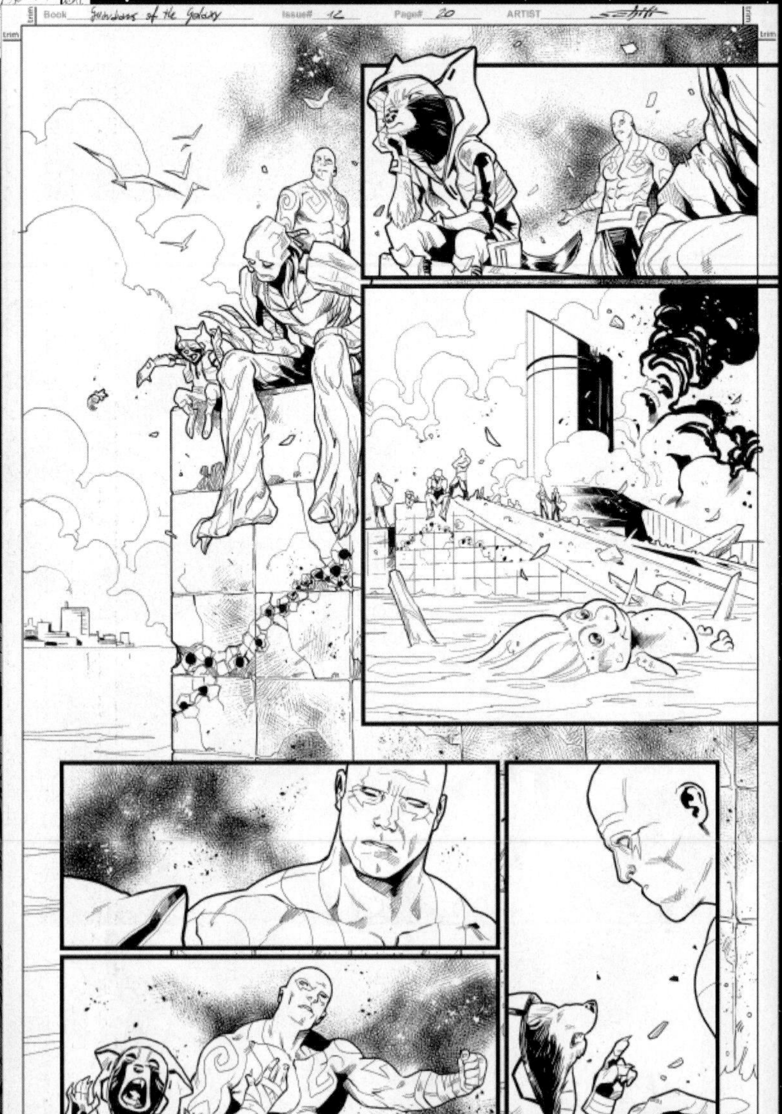
Book
Issue#
Page#
ARTIST
trim

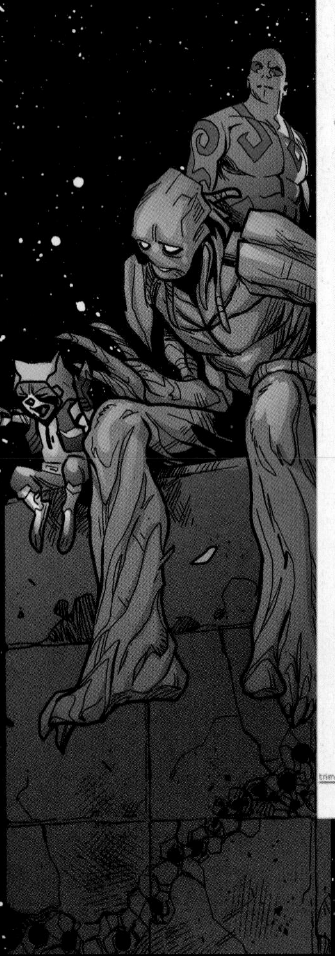

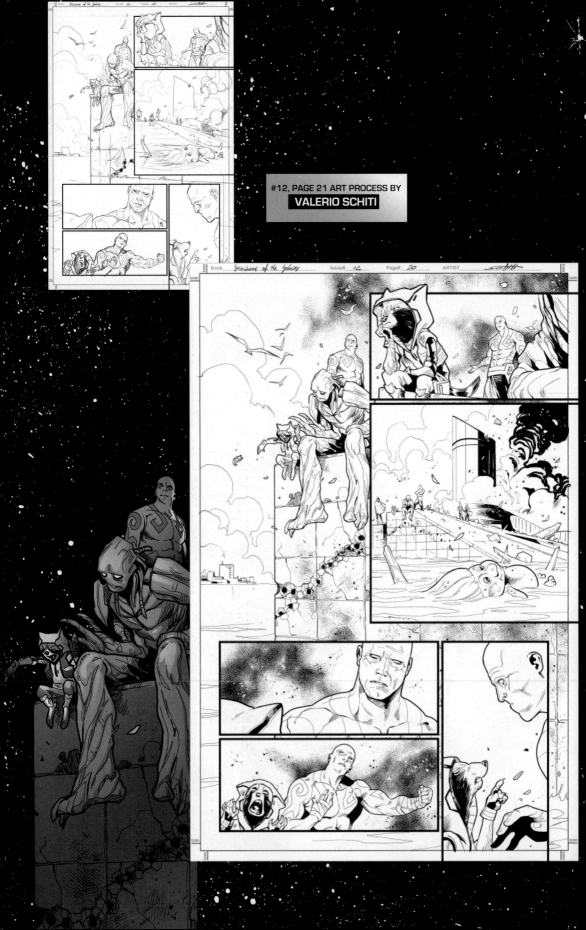

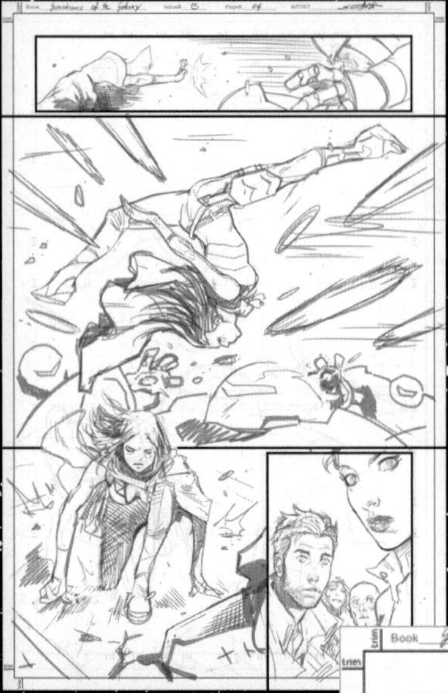

#13, PAGE 3 ART PROCESS BY

VALERIO SCHITI

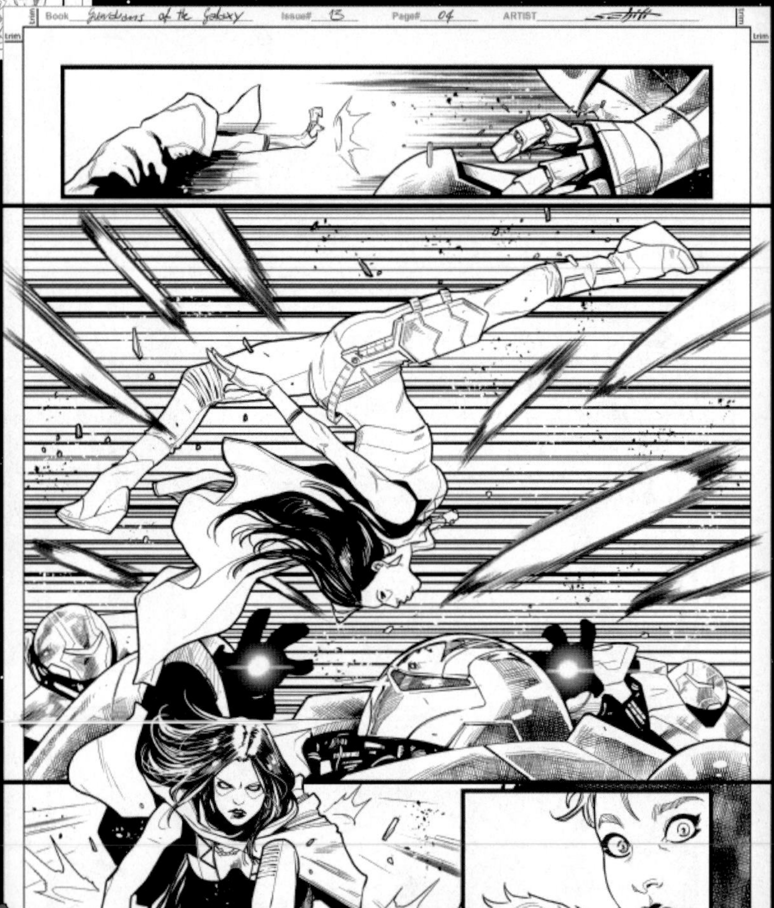
Book Guardians of the Galaxy Issue# 13 Page# 04 ARTIST

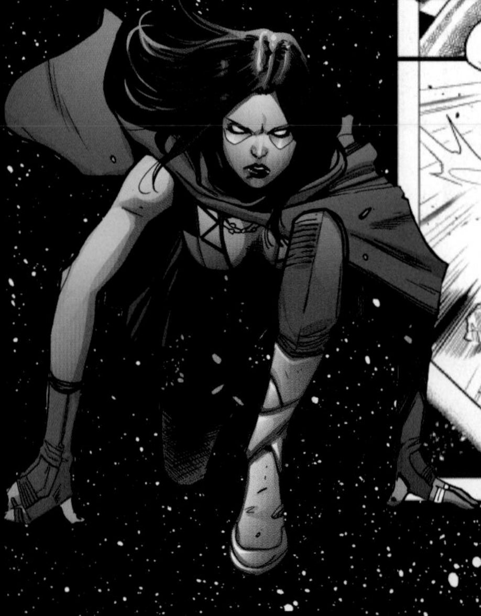

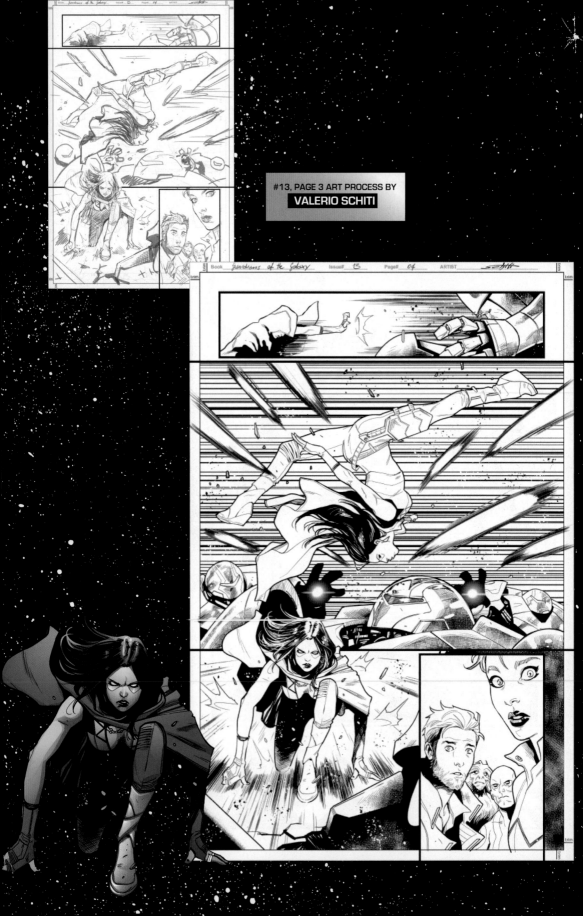

#13, PAGE 4 ART PROCESS BY
VALERIO SCHITI

#13, PAGE 8 ART PROCESS BY
VALERIO SCHITI

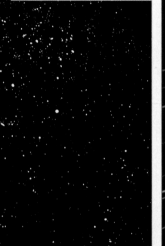

#13, PAGE 10 ART PROCESS BY
VALERIO SCHITI

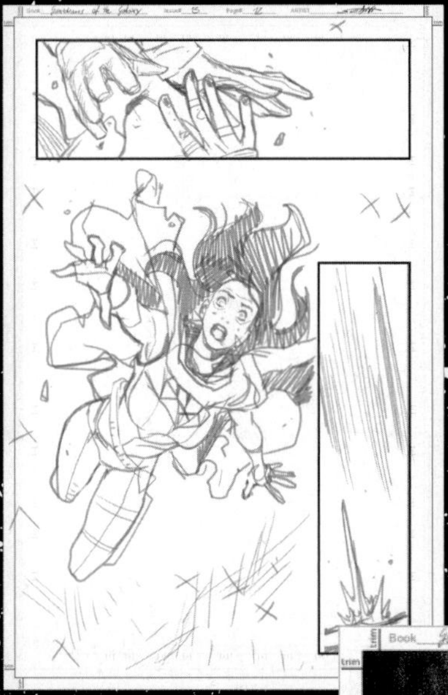

#13, PAGE 11 ART PROCESS BY

VALERIO SCHITI

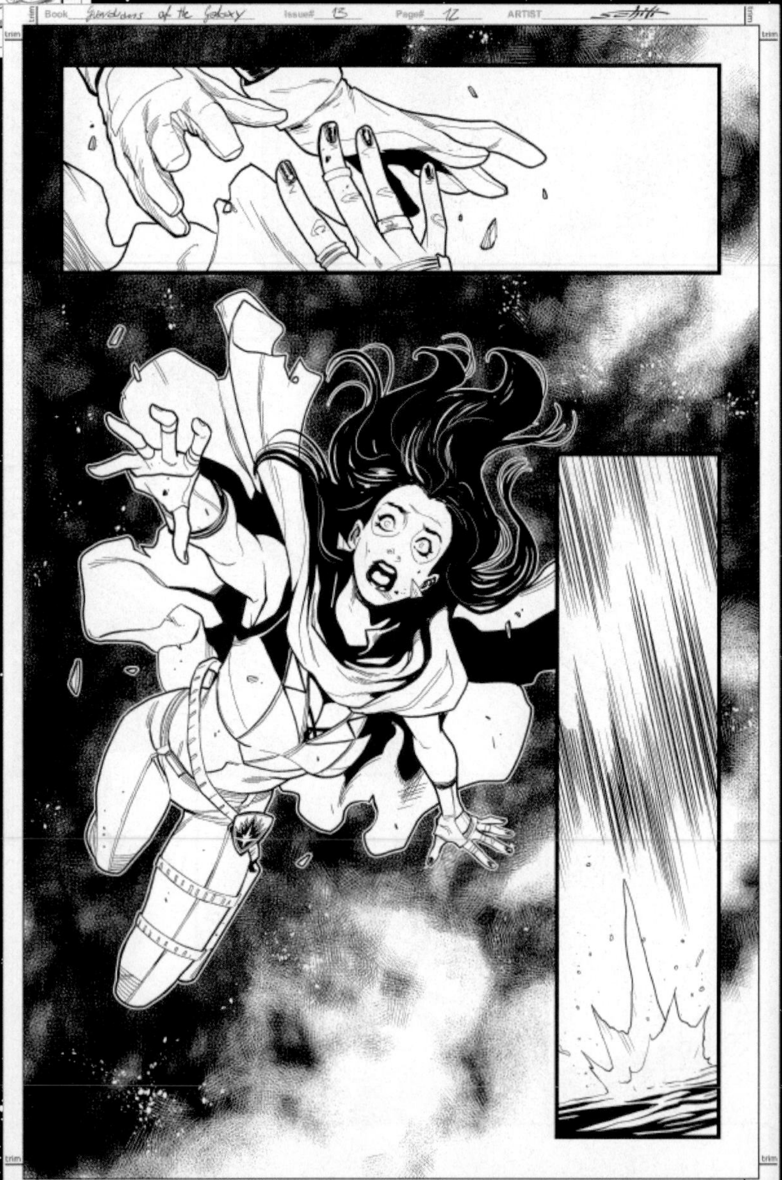
Book Guardians of the Galaxy Issue# 13 Page# 12 ARTIST

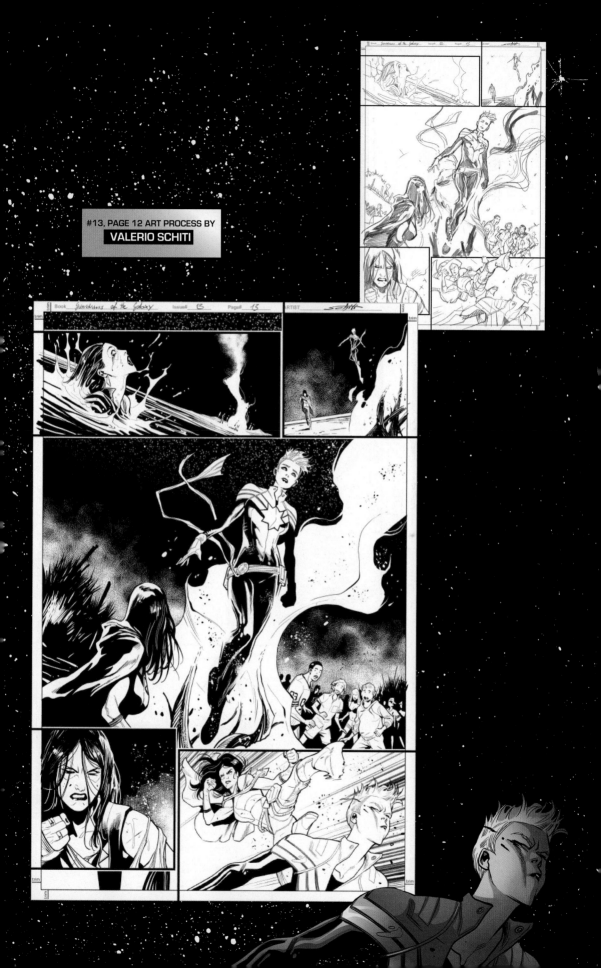

#13, PAGE 12 ART PROCESS BY
VALERIO SCHITI

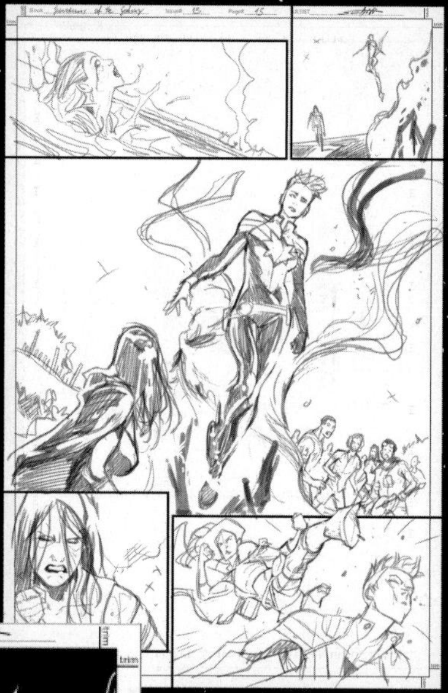

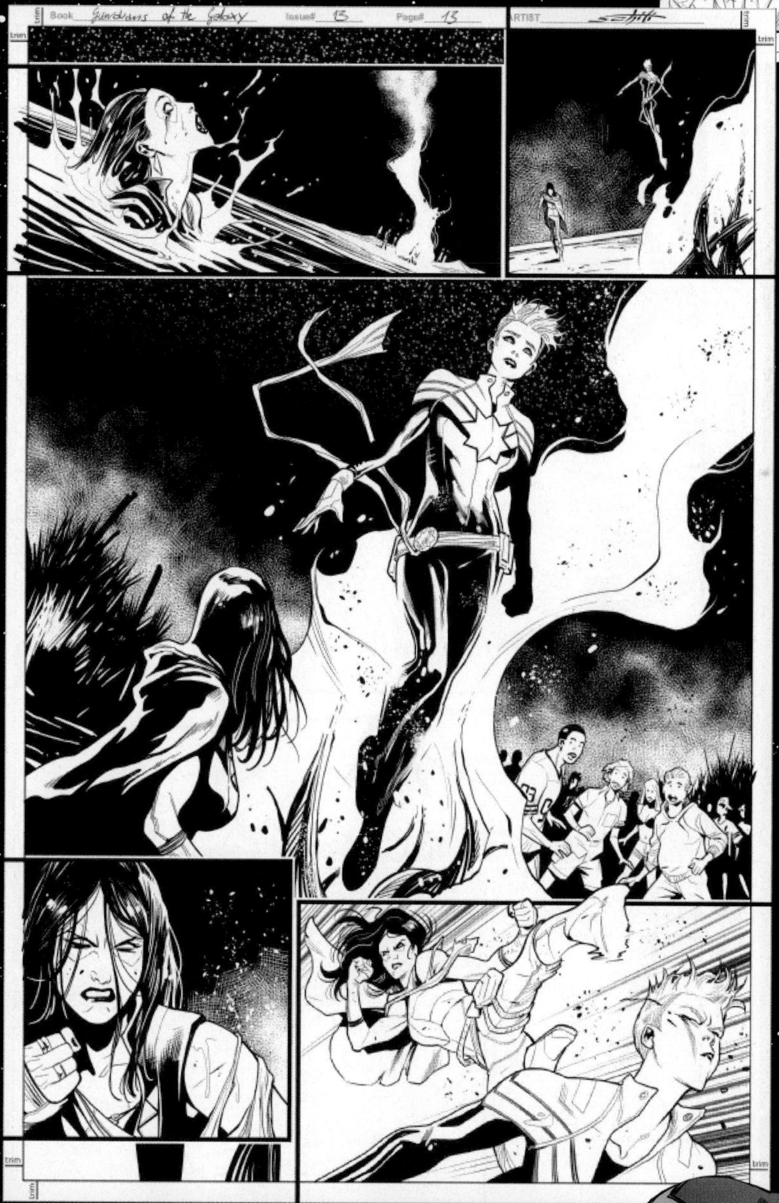

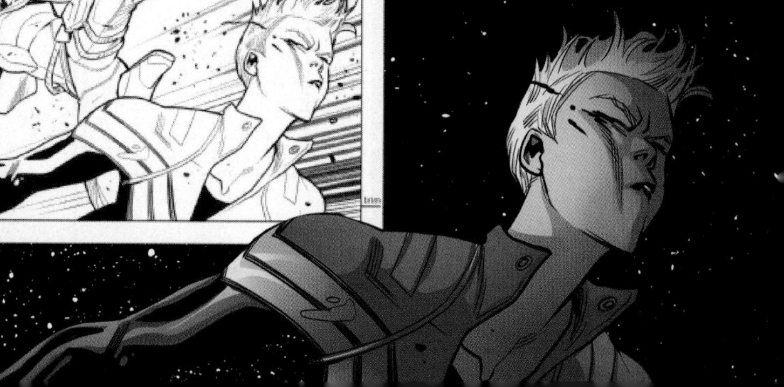

#13, PAGE 13 ART PROCESS BY
VALERIO SCHITI

#13, PAGE 14 ART PROCESS BY

VALERIO SCHITI

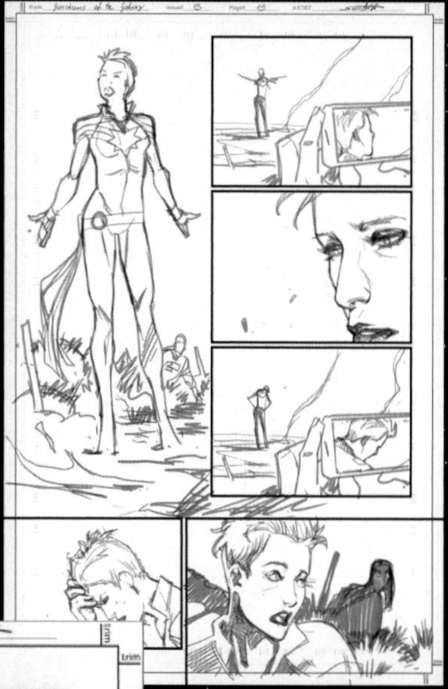

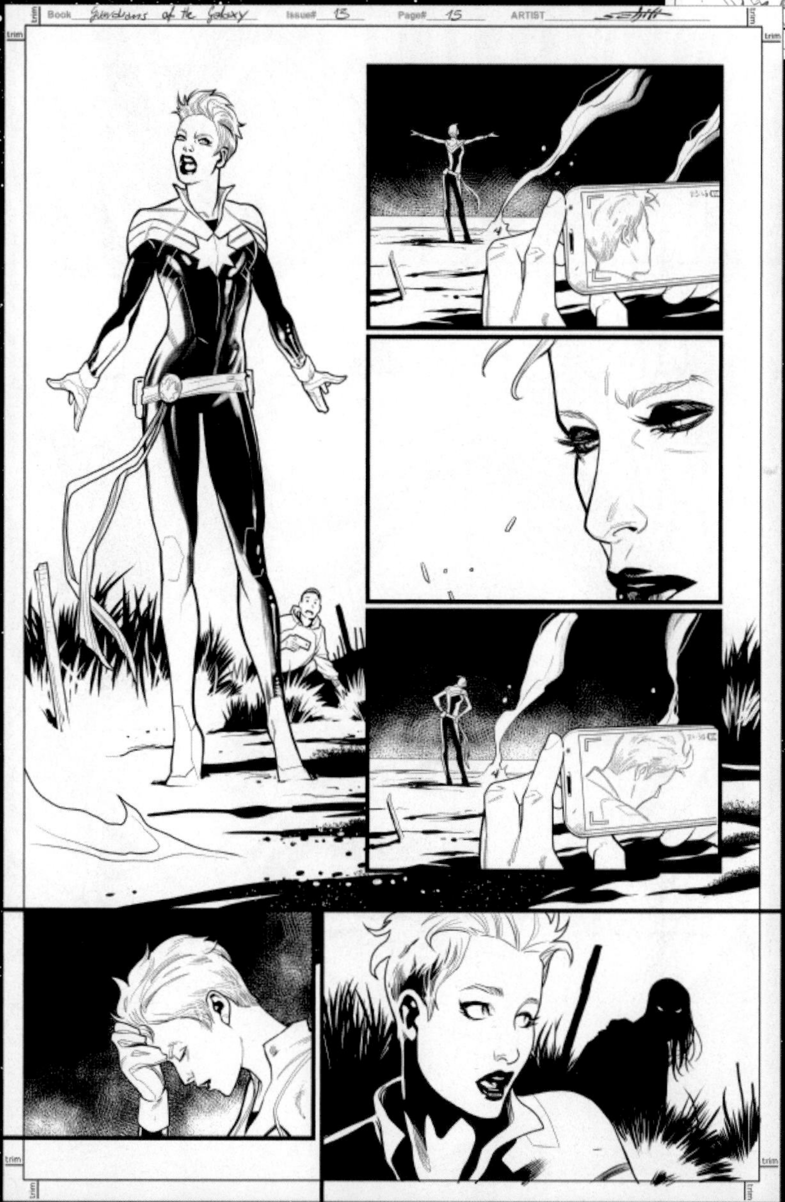

Book Guardians of the Galaxy Issue# 13 Page# 15 ARTIST
trim

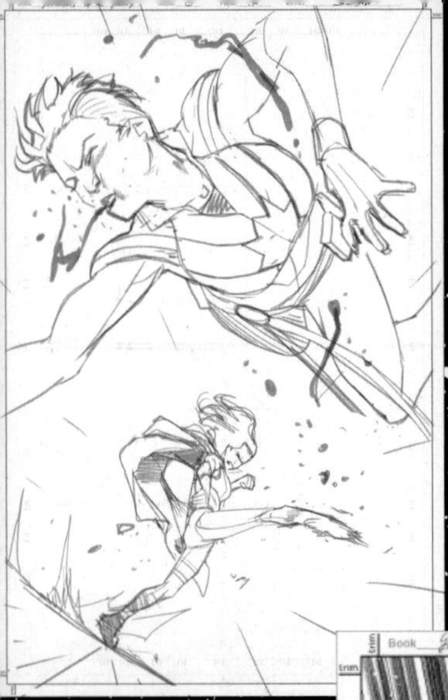

#13, PAGE 16 ART PROCESS BY

VALERIO SCHITI

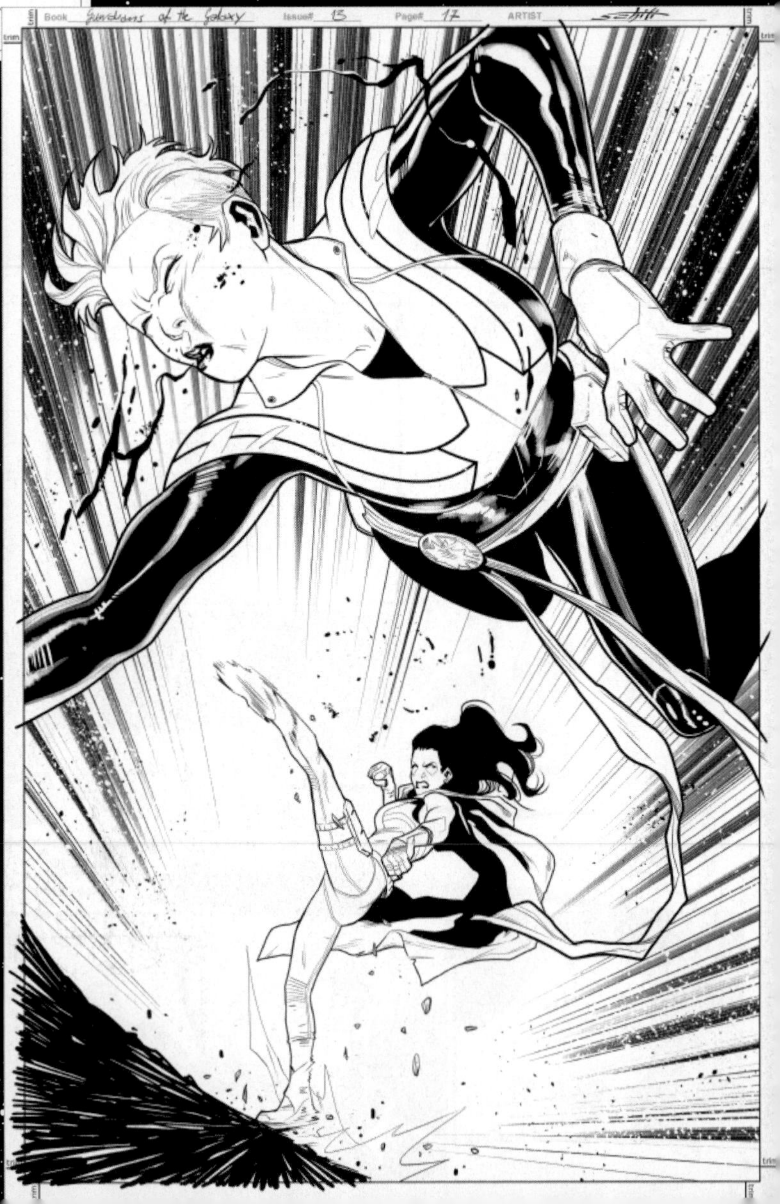
Issue# 13
Page# 17
ARTIST

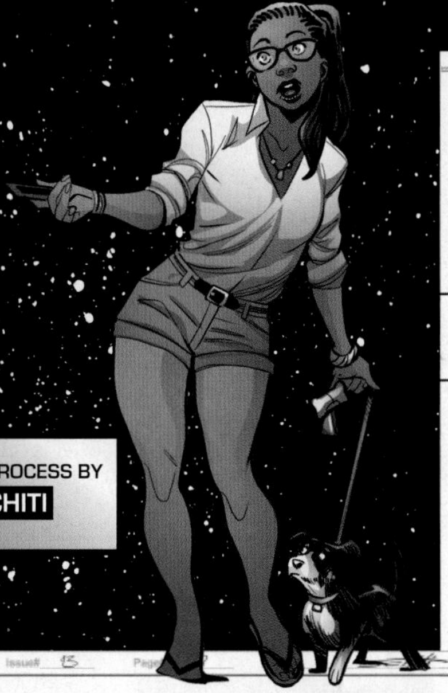

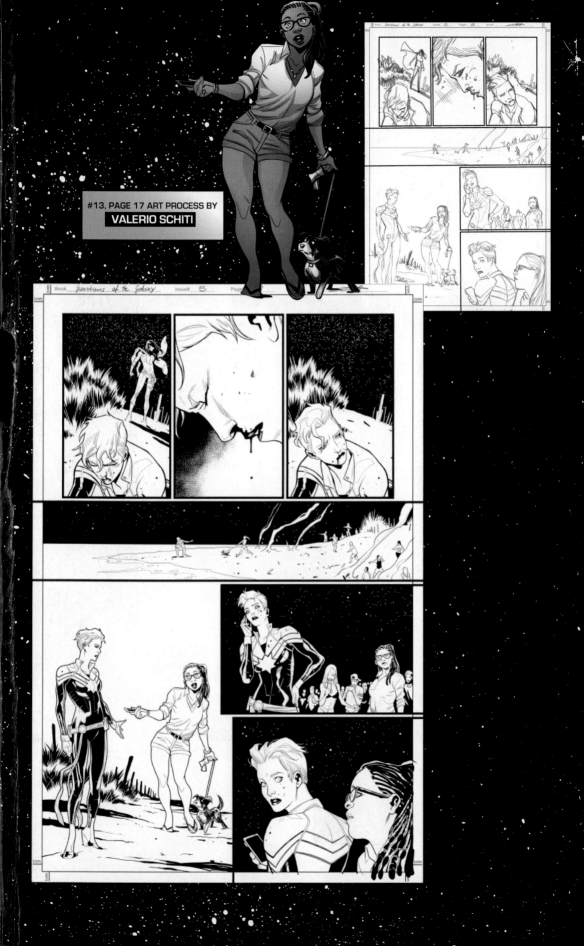

#13, PAGE 17 ART PROCESS BY
VALERIO SCHITI

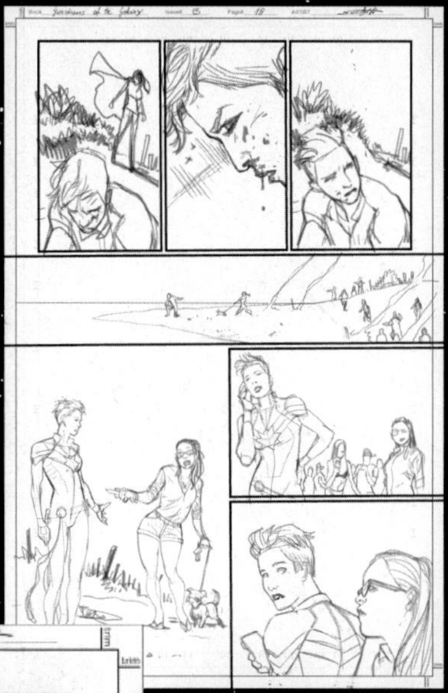

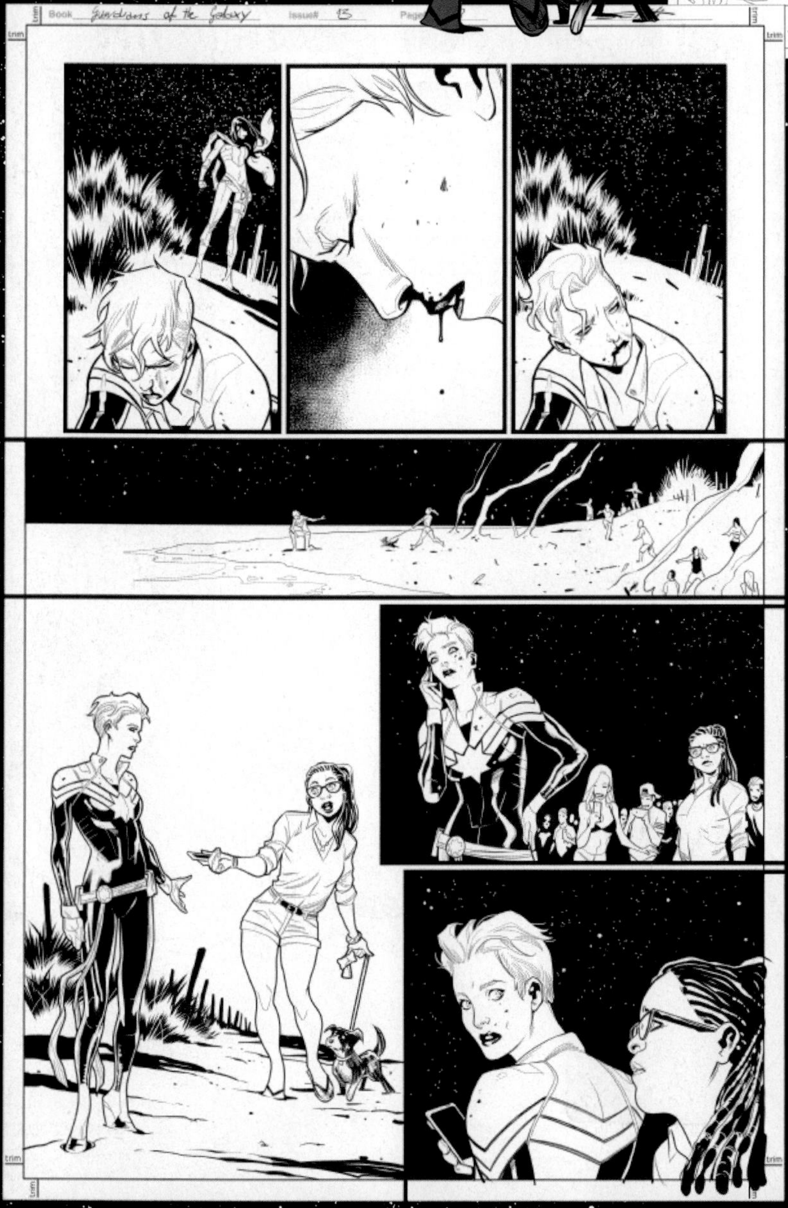

FREE
DIGITAL COPY

TO REDEEM YOUR CODE FOR A FREE DIGITAL COPY:

1. GO TO MARVEL.COM/REDEEM. OFFER EXPIRES ON 2/15/19.

2. FOLLOW THE ON-SCREEN INSTRUCTIONS TO REDEEM YOUR DIGITAL COPY.

3. LAUNCH THE MARVEL COMICS APP TO READ YOUR COMIC NOW.

4. YOUR DIGITAL COPY WILL BE FOUND UNDER THE 'MY COMICS' TAB.

5. READ AND ENJOY.

YOUR FREE DIGITAL COPY WILL BE AVAILABLE ON:
MARVEL COMICS APP FOR APPLE IOS® DEVICES
MARVEL COMICS APP FOR ANDROID™ DEVICES

DIGITAL COPY REQUIRES PURCHASE OF A PRINT COPY. DOWNLOAD CODE VALID FOR ONE USE ONLY. DIGITAL COPY AVAILABLE ON THE DATE PRINTCOPY IS AVAILABLE. AVAILABILITY TIME OF THE DIGITAL COPY MAY VARY ON THE DATE OF RELEASE. TM AND © MARVEL AND SUBS. APPLE IS A TRADEMARK OF APPLE INC., REGISTERED IN THE U. S. AND OTHER COUNTRIES. ANDROID IS A TRADEMARK OF GOOGLE INC.

MARVEL
FREE DIGITAL
COPY OFFER

PEEL HERE TO REVEAL CODE ➡